Prepared by the SPECIAL PUBLICATIONS DIVISION
NATIONAL GEOGRAPHIC SOCIETY, WASHINGTON, D.C.

SPLENDORS

SPLENDORS OF THE PAST: Lost Cities of the Ancient World

Contributing Authors: JOHN CARSWELL, LOUIS DE LA HABA,
  SEYMOUR L. FISHBEIN, THOMAS O'NEILL, CYNTHIA RUSS RAMSAY

Contributing Photographers: MEHMET BIBER, IRA BLOCK,
  VICTOR R. BOSWELL, JR., DAVID HISER, MICHAEL S. YAMASHITA

Contributing Illustrators: DAVID BLOSSOM, LLOYD K. TOWNSEND

Published by
  The National Geographic Society
  GILBERT M. GROSVENOR, *President*
  MELVIN M. PAYNE, *Chairman of the Board*
  OWEN R. ANDERSON, *Executive Vice President*
  ROBERT L. BREEDEN, *Vice President, Publications and Educational Media*

Prepared by
  The Special Publications Division
  DONALD J. CRUMP, *Editor*
  PHILIP B. SILCOTT, *Associate Editor*
  WILLIAM L. ALLEN, WILLIAM R. GRAY, *Senior Editors*

Staff for this Book
  MERRILL WINDSOR, *Managing Editor*
  CHARLES E. HERRON, *Picture Editor*
  CINDA ROSE, *Art Director*
  MARIANNE R. KOSZORUS, *Associate Art Director*
  PATRICIA F. FRAKES, JANE L. MATTESON, MARILYN L. WILBUR,
    Researchers; STEPHEN J. HUBBARD, *Assistant Researcher*
  LOUIS DE LA HABA, SEYMOUR L. FISHBEIN, PAUL D. MARTIN,
    JENNIFER C. URQUHART, MARILYN L. WILBUR,
    MICHAEL WINDSOR, *Picture Legend Writers*
  JODY BOLT, SUEZ B. KEHL, *Consulting Art Directors*
  RICHARD FLETCHER, CYNTHIA B. SCUDDER, *Assistant Designers*
  D. RANDY YOUNG, *Design Assistant*
  JOHN D. GARST, JR., VIRGINIA L. BAZA, SUSANAH B. BROWN,
    PATRICIA K. CANTLAY, GARY JOHNSON, ALFRED L. ZEBARTH,
    Map Research, Design, and Production

Engraving, Printing, and Product Manufacture
  ROBERT W. MESSER, *Manager*
  GEORGE V. WHITE, *Production Manager*
  DAVID V. SHOWERS, *Production Project Manager*
  MARK R. DUNLEVY, RICHARD A. McCLURE,
    RAJA D. MURSHED, CHRISTINE A. ROBERTS, GREGORY STORER,
    Assistant Production Managers
  MARY A. BENNETT, KATHERINE H. DONOHUE,
    Production Staff Assistants
  DEBRA A. ANTONINI, NANCY F. BERRY, PAMELA A. BLACK,
    BARBARA BRICKS, NETTIE BURKE, JANE H. BUXTON,
    MARY ELIZABETH DAVIS, CLAIRE M. DOIG,
    ROSAMUND GARNER, VICTORIA D. GARRETT,
    NANCY J. HARVEY, JOAN HURST, SUZANNE J. JACOBSON,
    ARTEMIS S. LAMPATHAKIS, VIRGINIA A. McCOY,
    MERRICK P. MURDOCK, CLEO PETROFF, VICTORIA I. PISCOPO,
    TAMMY PRESLEY, JANE F. RAY, CAROL A. ROCHELEAU,
    KATHERYN M. SLOCUM, JENNY TAKACS, *Staff Assistants*
  MARTHA K. HIGHTOWER, *Index*

Library of Congress CIP Data: page 295

*Masked entertainers play a double flute, finger cymbals, and
a large tambourine in this mosaic (shown approximately
actual size) from the ruins of Pompeii, Italy.* PAGES 2-3: *Jungle
growth intrudes on Angkor, capital of an empire that ruled
in Southeast Asia for more than 400 years.* PAGE 1: *Monks visit
a colossal figure of the Buddha at a remote grotto in Sri Lanka.*
ENDPAPERS: *In a 160-foot-long carving at Angkor, Khmer gods*
(FRONT) *and demons* (BACK) *churn the Sea of Milk with the
serpent body of the god Vasuki to create an elixir of immortality.*
HARDCOVER: *Female deities link arms on the wall of a library of
Angkor Wat. Elaborate coiffures and embroidered cloth reflect
the tastes of 12th-century Cambodian aristocrats.*

RIGHT: VICTOR R. BOSWELL, JR.; PAGES 2-3: PAOLO KOCH/RAPHO; PAGE 1: DAVID HISER;
ENDPAPERS: BERNARD P. GROSLIER; HARDCOVER: BASED ON PHOTOGRAPH BY GEORG GERSTER

Foreword

Most of us, I am sure, have shared the common experience of pausing to ponder a weathered, abandoned farmhouse, its roof swayed, its doors and windows gaping—or perhaps, as hikers, of coming upon a crumbling chimney standing sentinel to an old foundation now barely visible through the encroaching brush. For a moment we wondered: Who lived here—and how long ago? One family or more? Was someone born here, and did someone also die? What was life like for these unknown predecessors? Why did they leave? Briefly, in our minds, we stepped back in time, half expecting to find answers to our silent queries.

On a far grander scale those questions reflect the theme of this book. The combined life spans of all those weathered old farmhouses and half-hidden foundations form but a tiny thread of time in the unfolding fabric of civilizations that have risen, flourished, then fallen into oblivion. For almost a century the National Geographic Society, in its magazine and in its books, has chronicled the findings of archaeologists and of its own writers as they studied the ruins of ancient sites. They sought and found answers to questions much like the ones we might have asked. They, too, stepped back in time; and from their curiosity and determined investigation has come much of our knowledge of ages long gone by.

For them, lonely temple columns and blocks of stone emerging from the earth evoked vivid images of human activity. Twenty years ago, when he reported in NATIONAL GEOGRAPHIC on dramatic new findings at Pompeii, Amedeo Maiuri wrote: ". . . Pompeii seems to me at times a living city. When one strolls through the streets past the excavated shops and the houses whose murals shine so brilliantly with the images of life, one half expects to hear a sudden roar from the crowd in the distant amphitheater or the rumble of chariot wheels echoing down a side street."

Over the years, more and more of the city buried by Vesuvius almost two millenniums ago has been unearthed. And for Thomas O'Neill, who writes in this book of Pompeii's ruins today, it conjures up much the same vision Maiuri knew: ". . . I walk the length of the Street of Abundance and end again at the Forum. . . . I have partaken of the serenity of a Roman ghost town . . . but I also sense . . . I have walked through a crowded bazaar. The drama and the activity of the town come easily to my mind."

Often other Geographic writers have seen life little changed amid ancient surroundings. The venerable W. Robert Moore, whose Geographic career spanned 36 years, found Cambodians two decades ago worshiping at the same splendid temples of Angkor as had their ancestors—temples abandoned for 500 years, then restored. "As I stood in one of the vast stone structures," he wrote, "watching the candle-bearing pilgrims and listening to the distant *poom-poom* of a native drum, I could almost forget that Angkor had ever been deserted."

Much more recently, and thousands of miles from Angkor, author Seymour Fishbein realized that he, too, was peering into the past as he studied a village of block-like houses in the Holy Land that looked much like the towns King Solomon would have known.

Through long months and years of painstaking research and interpretation, scientists have literally pieced together answers to questions posed by mute walls and columns. And so it is today. In our chapter on the Kingdom of Kush, for example, you will find archaeologist Friedrich W. Hinkel laboring under a scorching African sun, restoring royal pyramids block by block, seeking clues to the mysterious civilization that once prospered there in the desert. "It's like working on giant jigsaw puzzles," Hinkel says, "with some parts gone forever."

Slowly, ever so slowly, out of ruins come reflections of everyday events. This book is but a chapter in a long, ongoing tradition of the National Geographic Society: to share with its members a glimpse into the lives and customs of ancient peoples—from Sumer, birthplace of writing and the wheel, to Hazor and Gezer and their Gates of Solomon, to the Great Temple at Hattusa in the land of the Hittites, to Sri Lanka, where worshipers offer flowers and prayers to Buddha just as their ancestors did hundreds of years ago.

In 1898 a Geographic author wrote of scientists who were slowly removing "the dust of centuries" at a site in the American Southwest. In the continuing quest for knowledge and understanding of our ancient forebears, National Geographic writers, photographers, editors, and researchers once again have joined archaeologists in sifting through "the dust of centuries" to reveal to you and your fellow Society members some of the world's greatest splendors of the past.

ROBERT L. BREEDEN
Vice President, Publications and Educational Media

Trained laborers remove sand from excavations at Nippur, sacred city of the Sumerians, where drifting dunes cause constant work. American excavation in Mesopotamia began at Nippur in 1888. The local workmen employed at those digs passed on their new skills to their sons. Today, the grandsons and great-grandsons continue the tradition.

Silhouetted against the sunset, a snaggletoothed row of timeworn pyramids studs a lonely ridge in the northern Sudan, mute reminders of a once mighty and still unfathomed civilization in the land of Kush.

Contents

MICHAEL S. YAMASHITA

By JOHN CARSWELL

AN INTRODUCTION:

Silence cloaks the great audience hall of Persepolis, ceremonial capital of ancient Persia. Among these soaring columns proud kings once received their subjects in regal splendor. Persepolis, built between 520 and 450 B.C., crowned one of the world's first great empires, a domain that reached from Egypt to India. Located in the southwestern part of present-day Iran, the city contained a magnificent array of residential and ceremonial structures — the finest built in Asia to that time.

PRECEDING PAGES: *Their procession forever locked in stone, dignitaries from Media ascend a stairway leading to a banquet hall. During the height of Persia's power, envoys from the empire's 23 conquered nations bore gifts to Persepolis each spring in tribute to their ruler. In 330 B.C. Alexander sacked and burned the city. By the first century B.C. the ruins of buildings, with their richly detailed reliefs and inscriptions, lay largely hidden by sand and debris. Not until the 1930s did archaeologists begin to excavate this lost city.*

What does one mean by a "lost city"? To my mind, the phrase conjures an image of some 19th-century explorer, struggling through dense jungle and suddenly stumbling upon the remains of an ancient civilization. Nor is this idea entirely fanciful, for some of the great discoveries of the past have been made in just such a romantic manner. One thinks of the Swiss explorer Johann Burckhardt who, guided by Bedouins, was the first outsider to reach the amazing Nabataean rock-cut city of Petra on the fringe of the Arabian desert. Or the German Heinrich Schliemann, who excavated the royal graves at Mycenae with their golden hoard of masks and jewelry, and sent his famous if inaccurate telegram: "I have gazed on the face of Agamemnon."

My own first encounter with a lost city was a different affair. In the 1950s I was working for a famous British archaeologist, Kathleen Kenyon, who was excavating ancient Jericho in the Jordan Valley just north of the Dead Sea. She had chosen the site in order to check certain interpretations of an earlier excavator, who claimed to have found the walls that collapsed at the sound of Joshua's trumpets. Quite early in the dig it became clear that the walls were much too old for the period of Joshua. Having determined this, Miss Kenyon continued down to find out what lay at the heart of the mound.

Jericho stands beside a perennial spring, traditionally said to be Elisha's well of the Old Testament. Today the spring still pours out a thousand gallons of water every minute, irrigating a fertile oasis, a vivid green blot in the dusty, arid plain of the Jordan Valley. The spring must always have attracted settlers, and over thousands of years the mound grew up beside it, the accumulation of the collapsed houses and debris of earlier inhabitants.

When I arrived at Jericho, I found that the excavation consisted of a series of strategically placed trenches cut from top to bottom of the mound. Miss Kenyon's plan was to correlate the levels and material from the several trenches and build up a chronological sequence of the periods of occupation at Jericho. The main trench was at the peak of the mound; here the later levels had been so eroded by wind and weather that our digging began in the middle Bronze Age.

In the main trench, an early town wall was soon exposed, and eventually no less than 17 phases of other town walls were revealed, indicating urban occupation over several thousand years.

Lower down, we reached Neolithic—late Stone Age—levels, where the inhabitants had occupied semiunderground houses, favored no doubt for their earthen insulation against the scorching summer heat of the floor of the valley. These people fashioned and used stone implements and bone tools, and also made primitive pottery vessels. Earlier still, even the pottery was absent; and it was at this level that, one Friday morning in 1953, a large stone circle appeared.

Brushing off the surface to photograph this curious feature, we found four stones at the center of the circle, set to define a square. The immediate reaction was that it was some sort of cult shrine, a common interpretation when archaeologists are confronted with some puzzling architectural feature. When we cleaned inside the square, however, we found a fifth stone a few inches down. Digging farther, we uncovered a sixth, then a seventh and an eighth, until it became clear that we were excavating an interior staircase. By now it was late in the day, and normally we would have stopped for the weekend. But the excitement was such that a break was out of the question.

Twenty-two steps down, we found ourselves at the bottom of the stairs and at the entrance of a horizontal passage, blocked by human skeletons. As the draftsman for the expedition, I was assigned to plot the bones before they were lifted. I spent that weekend drawing the remains of our Stone Age ancestors, who apparently had died violently in some desperate defensive action against an unknown invader.

The next move was to clear the outside of the stone circle. This revealed that the circle was in fact the top course of a massive stone tower, built against the inside of a town wall; outside the wall was a rock-cut ditch, nine feet deep.

All these defensive structures could be dated to the pre-pottery Neolithic period, at least 8000 B.C.—several thousand years before the introduction of masonry architecture in ancient Egypt. The town wall was traced at other parts of the site as well, and the team estimated that the pre-pottery settlement covered about ten acres and housed a population of at least two thousand. The evidence was clear: Jericho can claim to be the earliest known town in the world.

With Jericho as an example, we should consider how such early towns must have evolved. For untold generations our ancestors had led a nomadic existence; but about 10,000 B.C.—several thousand years after the end of the last Ice Age—a revolution in everyday life took place. Until then, people had lived in caves or open campsites and subsisted on a hunting-and-gathering economy. The great change took place with the advent of agriculture. Grown in sufficient quantities, grains and other cultivated products could provide a food surplus, eliminating the need for men to be always on the move in search of fresh prey.

This switch from a nomadic hunting to a settled farming economy can be traced in the lowest levels at Jericho; and the evidence from Jericho bridged the gap, for the first time, between our prehistoric ancestors and our own historic past.

With the development of a settled economy there must also have been a restructuring of society. Now the

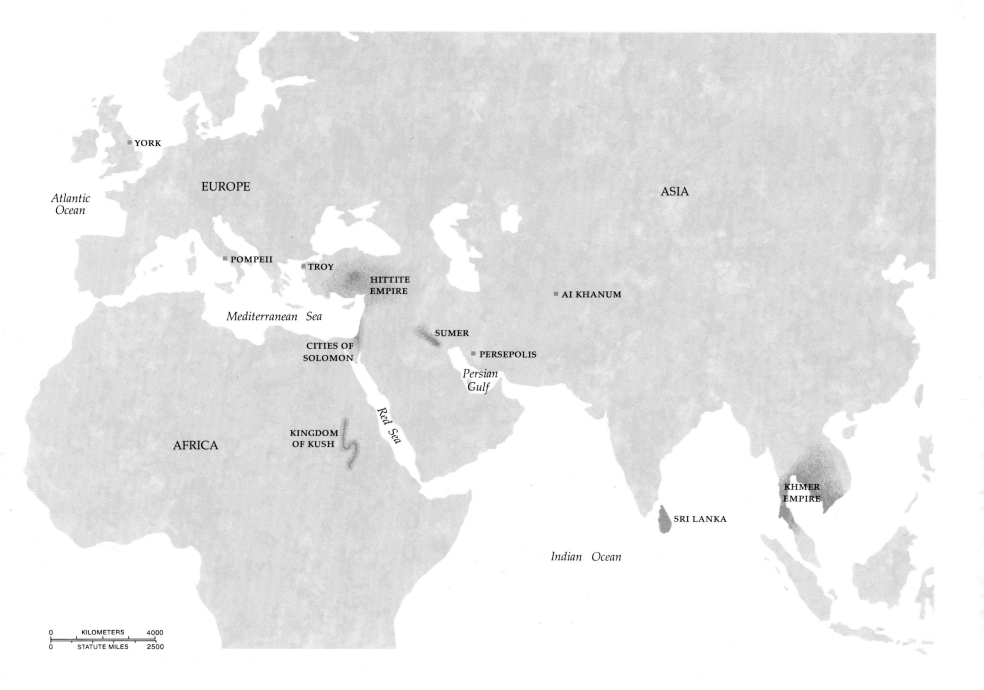

YORK

EUROPE

ASIA

Atlantic
Ocean

POMPEII

TROY

HITTITE
EMPIRE

AI KHANUM

Mediterranean Sea

SUMER

CITIES OF
SOLOMON

PERSEPOLIS

Persian
Gulf

Red Sea

KINGDOM
OF KUSH

AFRICA

KHMER
EMPIRE

SRI LANKA

Indian Ocean

KILOMETERS 4000
0
0 STATUTE MILES 2500

entire labor force was concentrated in one spot, and the opportunity arose for a much greater diversification of effort. Some workers would have been occupied primarily with the sowing and harvesting of crops, but the new stability would have released others to develop special skills, such as the production of tools and artifacts. The evidence of workshops from several Neolithic sites shows that this indeed was so. Within the settlements, different kinds of activity were localized in different areas. It was the logical disposition of these activities that led to the organization of urban society and the creation of towns.

But no sooner had mankind evolved towns and cities in which to live than these communities began to disappear. How does a city get lost?

It may be the result of a natural disaster—a great flood or a volcanic eruption, an earthquake or a lightning-caused fire racing out of control. More often, cities have been destroyed by human beings intent on

How do cities disappear? How are they found again? To help answer such questions, archaeologists patiently pursue their scholarly detective work, unraveling and interpreting the secrets of lost cities, lost kingdoms, lost civilizations. The sites and areas identified here—from Viking Jorvik at York in Great Britain to the spectacular legacies of the Khmer Empire in Southeast Asia—all figure in the story of the continuing search as set forth in this volume: some as brief citations, most as the subjects of entire chapters.

pillage and conquest. Such was the fate of Persepolis, put to the torch by Alexander the Great.

Cities may cease to function for less spectacular reasons, such as economic decline. The pattern of trade changes, and there is no longer sufficient stimulus to make the community prosper. In northern Syria, for instance, there are remains of more than 200 towns that were abandoned in the fifth century. No one ever returned to live in the area, and the buildings were never robbed of their stones. I have visited some of these ghostly places, and it is an eerie feeling to move from one abandoned site to another with its houses, churches, and caravansaries still standing two or three stories high.

The recovery of lost towns and cities is the work of the archaeologist, and over the years I have learned that there are as many methods of doing this as there are different kinds of urban complexes. The excavation of a town provides much more than a collection of interesting objects. It can demonstrate just how an unfamiliar society worked, not only by tracing the layout of buildings and streets but also by supplying details of the function and history of individual structures. The meticulous examination of such humble remains as garbage pits and drains will reveal much about the everyday life of the citizens, how they lived, what they ate and wore, and what kind of work they did. The evidence of religious structures can tell us, from a time long before written records were made, what kind of gods were worshiped, and what our ancestors' attitudes were toward death and eternity.

In the last century there has been much debate on the technique of excavating urban sites, and, broadly speaking, there has been a shift from a purely material interpretation of the evidence toward a more sociological approach. Excavations now tend to be the work of a team of highly skilled specialists rather than of one individual, each member applying a particular skill to a different facet of the work.

In the past there were attempts to dig whole towns, a level at a time, so as to give a complete plan. But with towns with a long history, this is almost impossible, for buildings often survive from one period to the next and become incorporated in the fabric of the later town. Furthermore, if you dig the whole town, each time you move down to an earlier

Reclaiming a living city's past, a trained archaeological volunteer carefully uncovers part of a wooden fence surrounding a tenth-century Viking house in York, England. Modern York sits atop ruins dating back to the founding of the city as a Roman stronghold nearly 2,000 years ago. Labels mark the location of every important find. The house turned out to be a coin-producing mint, the only one of its period excavated thus far in Britain.

phase you have to remove the upper level. However carefully you record the material, as the famous archaeologist Sir Mortimer Wheeler pointed out, "At the best, excavation is destruction."

A more practical approach, most commonly practiced today, is to dig a series of trenches at different points and link the evidence from each with the others to build up a composite picture of the site. This technique allows for future generations of archaeologists, with methods more advanced than our own, to excavate further and draw fresh conclusions. On the other hand, the disadvantage of partial excavation means that we never know the whole story. For instance, only one pre-pottery stone tower was excavated at Jericho —and we still do not know if it was unique or just one of a series of towers built against the town wall.

One site that was dug with the overall picture very much in mind was ancient Ur, in Iraq. Regardless of how much the methods used might be criticized today, there is no doubt that the excavations gave us a highly detailed insight into a civilization going back to the fourth millennium B.C., while also revealing the existence of an even earlier culture given the name Ubaid.

Ur was situated on the Euphrates River about halfway between Baghdad and the Persian Gulf. The archaeological site was first identified as the Ur of the Old Testament — the home of Abraham — by J. E. Taylor, who dug there on behalf of the British Museum in 1853-54. Further work led to a major excavation from 1922 to 1934 under the direction of British archaeologist Sir Leonard Woolley. One of Woolley's principal finds was a layer of mud eight feet thick separating the earlier from the later Sumerian town. To Woolley this was visible evidence of the flood described not only in the Old Testament story of Noah but also in Sumerian texts. It was "a vast flood in the valley of the Tigris and the Euphrates which drowned the whole of the habitable land between the mountains and the desert; for the people who lived there that was the world. . . . No wonder that they saw in this disaster . . . punishment of a sinful generation . . . and if some household had managed to escape by boat . . . the head of it would naturally be chosen as the hero of the saga."

Above the flood level and just outside the walls of the town, Woolley made his greatest discovery: the royal tombs of Ur. They contained an incredible richness of material, including gold and silver weapons, vessels, and jewelry; musical instruments and gaming boards; model boats and animal statues.

In front of the royal graves were the great death pits, lined with dozens of bodies of servants and courtiers. Woolley's excavation gave an awesome indication of the spectacular funeral rites that accompanied the

*B*uildings of modern York surround a midcity site known as Coppergate, the Viking name for "street of the woodworkers." Coppergate contains the timber walls of Viking workshops preserved for a thousand years by the moist clay subsoil. Excavations reveal Viking York, or Jorvik, as a flourishing commercial center populated by craftsmen and traders, but a rather untidy place: Two-thirds of this site comprises the remains of garbage pits.

Student at the York Archaeological Trust's Conservation Laboratory repairs a Viking pot, while a staff technician resews a medieval leather boot. Both of the rare artifacts came from Coppergate. Carefully freeze-dried by a new process, the well-preserved boot needed only a few stitches.

royal burials. But in addition to the graves of the rulers, Woolley dug those of ordinary individuals, and from their contents he was able to reconstruct some of the details of everyday life in the Sumerian period. Cemeteries are especially important to the archaeologist, for the recovery of whole objects from tombs supplements what is often found only in fragmentary form from the ruins of the city itself.

Although its location was known, Ur was a lost city in that it was a shapeless mass of decayed mud brick until Woolley excavated and analyzed the plan of the great ziggurat, the temples and the town walls, and worked out the sequence of its history. But sometimes the existence of a city is known, even if its exact location has been lost.

This was the case with Ai Khanum, a Greek colony on the frontier of Afghanistan. After the eastern campaigns of Alexander the Great, many Greek colonies were established in the eastern regions, and for years archaeologists have speculated on their exact location. Discoveries of Greek silver coins in Iran and Afghanistan and the obvious influence of classical Greek art on Kushan art and Ghandaran sculpture in northern India spurred French archaeologists working in Afghanistan to look for a Greek colony there. Finding not a single clue to any structure, they came to the conclusion that the Greeks must have been living in some kind of simple settlement, the traces of which had completely disappeared.

That judgment was suddenly reversed in 1962 when some peasants in a northern province of Afghanistan sold a finely carved Corinthian capital to Sarwar Nasher, the director of a cotton factory. Recognizing the significance of the stone, he immediately sent photographs to the French archaeologist Daniel Schlumberger. The French traced the find to a spot in the shadow of the snowcapped Pamir Mountains of the Soviet Union at the confluence of the Amu Darya (Oxus) and Kokcha Rivers. Here was the lost Greek city the archaeologists had sought for so long.

Professor Paul Bernard, director of the French Archaeological Delegation, proceeded to dig the Ai Khanum site for 15 years; but he emphasizes that he excavated only a small part of what is there.

Ai Khanum is partially located on a natural acropolis and covers at least a square mile; gentle folds in the ground indicate the plan of the classical Greek city below the surface. As Professor Bernard says, "Nothing was known of the material civilization of these Greek colonists in Central Asia, and we wanted to have a sample of every type of architectural structure."

The search has not been a simple one. The stone decoration of the buildings had greatly suffered from local pillagers who, as soon as the Greek settlers had been forced to abandon their city by invasions of nomads, had smashed the columns and pilasters to recover the metal clamps and burn the limestone into plaster. But most of the walls built of mud brick had survived, buried under the earth of their decayed upper structures; and the impressive remains of the royal palace, the gymnasium, the theater, the temples, and the private houses bear graphic witness to the grandeur of the dead city.

"What our excavation revealed was ample evidence of Ai Khanum as a flourishing administrative center, the capital of an entire province, where the government as well as the aristocracy of high civil servants and rich landowners had used public and private architecture as a declaration of their supremacy," Bernard explains. "The richness of the architectural decoration with its Greek columns, the existence of a local school of sculptors, the flourishing handicrafts, all were destined to have a lasting effect on subsequent local cultures.

"The treasury had also contained the reserve of currency. Most of the coins had been stolen, but the vases that held them, although broken, had survived; they were identified by Greek inscriptions that indicated the sum deposited in each."

*T*housands of miles away to the west, another colony of a different sort has recently been excavated in the British Isles. To visit it in the summer of 1980, I took the train northward from London to York, where a team of archaeologists is excavating Jorvik, the Viking colony long known to exist under the modern city. In this case the later town not only concealed the earlier Viking settlement but also prevented its excavation.

Since World War II, however, the extensive redevelopment of York has allowed the excavation of Viking remains, along with evidence of Roman, Anglian, and medieval English towns on the same site. For this purpose the York Archaeological Trust was formed in 1972, under the direction of Peter Addyman. It is conducting one of the most extensive and scrupulously organized large-scale excavations in all of Great Britain. Amid the bustling everyday life of the cathedral town, a whole series of digs is going on.

Like Ai Khanum, York was built at the junction of two rivers, in this case the Ouse and the Foss. The River Ouse is navigable all the way from the North Sea

Gesturing across the plain of Troy, the visionary 19th-century archaeologist Heinrich Schliemann locates scenes from the Iliad *for his wife, Sophia. Accepting Homer's poetic description as historical fact, he concluded the ancient city lay beneath this hill in northwestern Turkey. Schliemann retired from business to pursue his dream, and he proved his theory. Here, and later at Mycenae, he made a series of pioneering discoveries of Bronze Age Greek culture.*

PAINTING BY LLOYD K. TOWNSEND

fifty miles away. Thus linked to the seaways, York became an important military base of the Romans; and Viking warriors sailed up the river to capture the town from the Angles in A.D. 866.

Until then, the Vikings had made their impact on Europe as raiders and pillagers, but as the ninth century waned they became increasingly interested in conquest and settlement. In their native Scandinavia there were few towns, and seizing the strategically located York, second largest city in England, gave them a valuable base for expanding trade. They also settled in villages in the countryside—many Yorkshire villages have Viking names — and for eighty years Jorvik itself was under the direct rule of the Scandinavian kings. The English finally threw out the last Norwegian prince, Eric Bloodaxe, in A.D. 954.

In 1976 a large renewal site became available for excavation at 16-22 Coppergate in York, right in the heart of the Viking town. This was the site I visited first, and here I met the field director, Richard Hall.

"Because York is low-lying and dampness from its two rivers seeps upward, there has always been a problem in building houses with cellars in the town," Richard said as we walked about. "Paradoxically, the dampness has resulted not in the rotting but actually in the preservation of much archaeological organic material; and the absence of cellars has also meant that the earlier town levels have not been dug away. It's only been in the last thirty years that modern construction methods and projects requiring deep foundations have threatened destruction of the archaeological deposits."

Digging at Coppergate under Hall's direction, workers have recovered all sorts of organic material—wood, cloth, leather, seeds—remarkably well preserved in the waterlogged soil. To deal with this material, the University of York has created a special Environmental Archaeology Unit comprising botanists, entomologists, soil scientists, and other specialists. There is also a Conservation Laboratory, which has evolved highly sophisticated techniques for preservation. Wooden objects, for instance, are initially kept wet in a sealed plastic bag with a fungicide, then freeze-dried in a vacuum to extract all moisture and leave the wood intact and dry.

Richard Hall's excavations turned out to be in the middle of the commercial quarter of the Viking town, under what is still the business center of modern York. So far, he and his workers (all experienced, trained archaeological students) have exposed four tenements, or separate lots. "Each tenement has a shop front on the street and a workshop behind," he said. "One was a woodworker's establishment where bowls and cups were turned on a lathe; even the wood

Still flowing steadily from a spring generally considered the biblical fountain of Elisha, cool water creates a verdant oasis in the Jordan Valley. The people of the world's first known permanent community, ancient Jericho, settled here; its mound rises seventy feet high between the grove of trees and the Mount of Temptation in the background. The mound grew as the occupants built new structures on ruins of the old. The earliest found, including the tower below, date from 8000 B.C.

FOLLOWING PAGES: *Sunlight washes over the mud houses of a new ruin at Jericho: a former Palestinian refugee camp, unoccupied since the Arab-Israeli war of 1967. Beyond the mound of the ancient settlement and the houses and trees of modern Jericho, the waters of the Dead Sea form a gray horizon.*

FOLLOWING PAGES: NATHAN BENN

OPPOSITE: JOHN CARSWELL; ABOVE: KATHLEEN KENYON

shavings have survived. Another was occupied by a jeweler who made pendants and rings of amber and jet. Bone and antler workers made combs and pins; and metalworkers cast silver ingots in soapstone molds." The shops also sold imported goods—soapstone from Scotland, sharpening stones of Norwegian schist, pottery wine vessels from Germany.

"The earliest houses had walls of wattle," Richard pointed out, "but later they were built partly underground, with walls of strong wooden planks. The wooden houses did not survive long, perhaps for thirty years; when the old houses fell or burned down or were relegated to use as refuse dumps, new ones were built on top. Because of this, the identification of different stages is immensely complicated."

I began to appreciate the complexity of the excavation when I learned that more than 23,000 posts and structural remains had been numbered. There had also been 7,900 small finds, including wooden objects, combs, pieces of jewelry and glass, and leather shoes. Each article had a separate card, with more than 60 details to be entered. In addition to all this, more than half a million fragments of pottery had been recovered. All this information has been computerized, along with much specialized background data, with the result that a picture of life in the Viking town is emerging to a degree of detail undreamed of till now.

From the animal bones we know what the Vikings ate. They kept cattle, pigs, sheep, chickens, geese, and ducks, hunted deer, and caught all sorts of fresh- and saltwater fish; they were also great oyster eaters.

As Peter Addyman, the director, has summed it up, "People were always aware that the Vikings were here, but we had no idea until quite recently just where their settlement was or what it looked like."

Another urban redevelopment, this time in Syria, led directly to my own excavation of a lost city far away in Sri Lanka. About 1960 the modernization of Damascus led to the demolishing of much of the old town, and many of the inhabitants moved into modern apartments. In the process people often sold surplus possessions, including family heirlooms; and as a result a large quantity of Chinese blue-and-white porcelain came onto the market.

I first saw pieces of this blue-and-white in, of all places, the Singer sewing-machine agency in Damascus. Women had been bringing it in to trade as part payment for new sewing machines. A few months later I found a 14th-century Chinese dish under a pair of old trousers in a second-hand clothes shop!

What started as a trickle of blue-and-white soon became a flood, and I decided to catalog as much of it as possible before it was dispersed abroad. In all I drew and photographed more than 800 pieces, mostly from the Yüan (1279-1368) or Ming (1368-1644) Dynasties. Early Arabic texts tell us that Chinese porcelain was always highly prized in the Near East, and excavations have produced a number of broken sherds of Chinese ware. But for several hundred pieces to have survived more or less intact was phenomenal.

In the process of cataloging the Chinese ware from Syria, I became interested in the routes by which it must have come to the Near East. Although some of it may have been carried overland by caravan through Central Asia, most of it must have come by sea.

I knew that in the Near East, fragments of Chinese porcelain have been found at Al Fustat (old Cairo), at Antioch, along the Red Sea coast, in south Arabia, in east Africa, and beside the Persian Gulf. It has also been excavated in quantity in the Far East in Java, Sumatra, and the Philippines. But as far as I know, no

one had really looked for Chinese porcelain in the lands between—that is, in India, Sri Lanka, and the islands of the Indian Ocean.

In 1974 I made my first expedition to this area to search for Chinese porcelain, visiting in particular the Maldive Islands. On the capital island of Male, 400 miles southwest of Sri Lanka, I discovered that the coral sand of this tiny isle was packed with sherds of Chinese pottery, ranging in vintage from 9th to 19th century—proving that the Maldives lay on the prevailing direct sea route from the Far East to the Near East.

Four years later in Sri Lanka, at the end of a survey of the island's ancient ports mentioned in Chinese and Arabic texts, I was lucky enough to find and excavate an entire shipload of Chinese porcelain that had been abandoned and buried in a dune sometime in the early 12th century. I was led to it by a Tamil boy who had come upon fragments while digging for building sand. From the thousands of sherds, I was able to reconstruct the forms of more than 500 Chinese vessels.

Encouraged by this find, I asked the Sri Lankan Department of Archaeology for permission to dig a site near Vankalai, at the northern tip of the island, where Chinese sherds could be seen lying on the surface. There my colleagues and I excavated a village in which Chinese ware was found side by side with sherds of Islamic pottery and masses of locally made earthenware. For the first time, we could compare ceramics from all three cultures — Chinese, Islamic, and Sri Lankan—with the hope of working out a chronological sequence for all three kinds of pottery.

But the village proved to have been one of limited duration, probably a period of not more than fifty years at the beginning of the 12th century. What we needed was a site reflecting a much longer time span, with a similar mixture of local and imported goods. The search led us to Mantai, just a few miles away; and it is this lost city I began to dig in the spring of 1980.

*M*antai is not a totally new discovery; its existence has been known since the late 19th century, and it has been dug sporadically. It is known too from old chronicles, having been mentioned as a famous city as early as the seventh century, and it is almost certainly the Persian outpost located on the island even earlier.

When I first visited the site in 1974, I found a great horseshoe-shaped mound surrounded by a double moat that still fills with water in the rainy season. It is partly covered with scrub jungle, and at its center is a famous Hindu temple to which come thousands of pilgrims from India every year.

The ground was littered with sherds of Chinese, Islamic, and local pottery, and on my first visit I was shown a carved stone that had been dug up; it was elegantly inscribed in foliated Kufic, a type of Arabic script that flourished in the Near East in the ninth century. When I returned in 1980 for a more careful survey, I made two soundings and found that there are archaeological deposits to a depth of more than thirty feet. The very top dates from the 11th century; at the bottom there is pottery of the Roman period.

What do we expect to find when large-scale excavation of this city starts in earnest? All indications are that Mantai not only was at the principal crossroads between India and Sri Lanka but also was the great central emporium for merchants from both the Near and the Far East. Arabs, Chinese, and Indians all traded at this city in the middle of the Indian Ocean.

I discovered that the very location of Mantai has a geological basis. India and Sri Lanka are joined by a chain of underwater reefs, known as Adam's Bridge, that prevent ships from passing through the narrows between the two countries. Ocean vessels would have been obliged to anchor on one side or the other, and then could exchange cargoes; and Mantai grew up at exactly the point where this exchange took place.

Mantai's symmetrical plan suggests a well-organized city. Most of the buildings were probably made of *kadjan* — palm leaves and mud—as they are today; but there must have been more substantial structures, for there is evidence of sturdy brick walls. We have located several stone-lined wells, doubtless the city's main source of fresh water.

Here we hope to find material of Hindu, Buddhist, and Islamic cultures, Chinese and Arabic, Indian and Roman. Mantai represents no single cultural tradition, but rather a melting pot of civilization that lasted more than a thousand years, a lost city of immense complexity and great potential rewards.

Mantai also is a sharp reminder that cities, unlike human beings, never completely disappear. Even in the atomic cataclysm at Hiroshima, one result of the searing impact of the bomb was to scorch the city plan on the devastated, suddenly vacant ground, while remains of blasted buildings marked the fringe like the edge of a tattered carpet. Cities always survive in one form or another, whether covered by desert or overgrown by jungle, concealed by later construction or simply forgotten by the world. Their hidden history lies waiting, to be brought to light by the archaeologist's spade and the curiosity of future generations.

Medallion of Cybele, found at Ai Khanum, bears an intricate illustration worked in chased silver plated with gold. Ten inches in diameter, the plaque reflects both Greek and Asiatic influences: Under the sun (personified as Helios), the moon, and a star, the Greek goddess of nature, Cybele, shares her chariot with a winged Victory; an attendant, humbly barefoot, holds over the riders a parasol in the Indian fashion.

*T*umbled columns of Ai Khanum's administrative center lie in random confusion. The Greeks supported the brick walls of the complex with more than a hundred limestone Corinthian columns. The Greek colonists abandoned Ai Khanum about 150 B.C. Later pillagers razed the center to recover the bricks inside the walls, and tore down the columns in search of the metal clamps used to hold the stones together. Two fragments of columns, found by peasants in 1962, led to the discovery of the city's location. Archaeologists excavating the site have found an architectural composition unlike any other in the Greek world. Elements of Oriental, Mesopotamian, and Persian origin blend freely here with traditional Hellenic motifs.

PAUL BERNARD

T̶ragile clues to the past, rare porcelains provide evidence of early trade between cities of the Near and the Far East. The three large Chinese Yüan Dynasty fragments, along with the four smaller fragments of Islamic copies, turned up in Egypt. Most of the Chinese porcelains displayed below them, photographed against the Mediterranean, came from Syria. At Mantai, in Sri Lanka, archaeologist Martha Prickett of Harvard's Peabody Museum checks details of a cross section of a sounding. Chinese pottery sherds appeared here also, confirming the use of a sea route from China as early as the ninth century A.D.

By Seymour L. Fishbein

THE SUMERIANS

"Only the gods live for ever. . . . As for mankind, numbered are their days, Whatever they achieve is but wind." Wisdom of ancient Sumer seems a fit epitaph for the weathered mound rising above the stark Mesopotamian plain. Yet here at Uruk—called Erech in the Bible, Warka in modern Iraq—lay inscribed clay tablets that evidenced mankind's enduring achievement of literacy. Some 5,000 years ago epic heroes of Uruk reigned

over "harmony-tongued Sumer." Majestic temple mounds, or ziggurats—such as this one honoring the goddess Inanna—linked earth to heaven for Sumerians. The western world has long associated ziggurats with the Tower of Babel; in Genesis the tower built "unto heaven" symbolized human presumption. As punishment, humanity lost its single harmonious language, replaced by a confusing babel of tongues. PAGES 34-35: *Worshipers set small figures in Sumerian temples as proxies. The stone supplicants stood with hands humbly clasped, faces frozen in wide-eyed rapture.*

ext question: "Do you know multiplication, reciprocals, coefficients, balancing of accounts, administrative accounting, how to make all kinds of pay allotments, divide property, and delimit shares of fields?"

The student's mind is blank. His limp alibi, though recorded on a drab clay tablet in wedge strokes of cuneiform that few of us can decipher, speaks across the centuries to anyone who has ever blown an exam: "I have never heard my master's words. You have not taught it to me."

The teacher would have none of it. "You are already an adult," he snapped, "really somewhat aging, and like an old ox you cannot be taught anymore."

In the course of his ordeal the student, a scribe trainee, was quizzed on pronouns and verb tenses, on the jargon of priests, jewelers, shepherds, and master shippers, and on singing and leading a choir.

"This is an examination," declared the *ummia*—school father, or teacher—at one point. "Don't scream, and don't get upset. Don't clear your throat constantly." Finally, he ended with these words: "Sit down and be humble to the scribal art. You have to ponder it night and day. The scribal art is a good lot. The scribe has a good protective spirit, and he has a clear eye, and that is what the royal palace needs."

The examination tablet, says its translator, Professor Åke Sjöberg of the University of Pennsylvania, dates from early in the first millennium B.C., but the wide-ranging curriculum and the practice of setting down "schooldays" dialogues pursue a tradition many centuries older. It reflects the precious legacy of the Sumerians who in ancient Mesopotamia—the alluvial plain cradled by the curving arms of the Tigris and Euphrates Rivers—established the earliest known society where people could read and write.

Though its gift of writing made possible the recording of history, Sumer itself was lost to history. Its successors in Mesopotamia—Babylonia and Assyria—have long been familiar through the chronicles of the Near East, notably as the hated conquerors of Israel and Judah in the Old Testament. But not until a century ago, after the triumphant decipherment of cuneiform writing, did the Sumerians emerge, distinguished by a language far different from the Semitic tongues of the Babylonians and Assyrians.

In the tablets that have come to light in our

VICTOR R. BOSWELL, JR.   TABLETS SHOWN APPROXIMATELY ACTUAL SIZE

GEORG GERSTER/PHOTO RESEARCHERS

Young Iraqi marsh dwellers learn English from a visiting teacher by waters that nurtured Sumer's civilization. Pupils then practiced wedgemanship (square tablets) or copied exercises—on the round tablet two neat model lines appear at top, the student's crude copy below. Cloth or knife could erase; the teacher's thumb could press out errors. Skilled hands today work delicately to dig such nuggets from the past.

Writing evolved to keep track of property, scholars theorize. Early on, clay envelopes with the owner's rolled seal held tokens for goods, such as cows. Later, drawn tokens appeared on tablets: 4 measures of barley, 5 cows. Then the direction of the writing changed, perhaps to avoid smudges. But scribing curves made for slow going; pictures gave way to lines pressed in with a wedge tip. The proverbial ideal: "A scribe whose hand moves as fast as the mouth, that's the scribe for you."

PAINTING BY LLOYD K. TOWNSEND

century, we find that school problems have not changed much in 4,000 years. We learn of nagging, ambitious parents and their jaded, underachieving children; of stern teachers and bullying monitors. Parents are not above buying a teacher's goodwill; pupils complain of only 6 free days a month, leaving 24 to be spent in class, and "long days they are."

The tablets also tell of a ruler's concern for justice, of price controls to keep the poor from being gouged. There are ledgers, lullabies, and legal codes, and the epic tales of the hero Gilgamesh who yearns for eternal life; and there is a story of a flood that destroyed humankind—except for one good man and his family.

Farmers of Sumer worked with plows, potters with wheels. Merchants built an empire of trade. With metal tools, artisans carved stone statues, cylinder seals, and jewelry. In all these things—in law and social reform, in literature and architecture, in commercial organization, and in technology—the achievements of the cities of Sumer are the earliest we know about.

They were actually city-states, separated by cultivated fields, reedy marshes, and desert, and they flourished along ancient channels of the Euphrates River and on canals dug to harness the river's unpredictable flow. The taming of the Tigris, a swifter, more turbulent stream, awaited the skills of a later era.

With time the Euphrates channels shifted. Today the river flows west of most Sumerian city sites, and these once great centers lie in silent ruins. They grace a modern Iraq troubled by war with neighboring Iran. Much of the ongoing field archaeology has marked time while the conflict wore on. So I explored ancient Sumer through the works and memories of men and women who have trenched into the buried cities, deciphered the tablets, revealed the treasures of mind and hand.

"It's a harsh and empty land," said Dr. Robert McCormick Adams as we talked at the University of Chicago's Oriental Institute, where he recently became the director. He had undertaken a years-long reconnaissance of Mesopotamian settlement patterns, and he was eager to return, though the field was not an easy one to explore. "It's bone dry," he said. Where dunes straddle the route "they utterly impede transportation. You can sink a vehicle in them."

In *Heartland of Cities,* his most recent book on his field surveys, Professor Adams writes: "To suggest the immediate impact of human life, there is only a rare tent, its mirage floating over the horizon . . . sometimes a small knot of women collecting dead scrub for firewood; and at long intervals a distant file of camels or a scattering of sheep and goats with their young herdsman." The storied desert hospitality lives on; pause at a village to ask directions, and someone wants to kill a sheep and make a feast.

"Towns today," writes Adams, "as always are

concealed by dense surrounding belts of palm groves. But sometimes, from a high dune on still, early mornings, one can detect them even from the remote desert as faint, spiky clusterings. . . . Just so wayfarers once must have taken their bearings on the turreted walls and ziggurats of much more ancient urban centers."

These cities appeared in Sumer around 3500 B.C. From the beginning they must have been trade centers as well. The land had the life-giving Euphrates, mud for making brick and pottery, reeds for weaving boats and houses—similar to those that transport and shelter the Marsh Arabs at the head of the Persian Gulf today. But Sumer had virtually no wood, no stone, no metals. By caravan and sail, the cities sent forth barley, wool and woolen cloth, hides, and linseed oil. From the mountains to the north, and beyond, came back lapis lazuli, copper, gold. From the lands of the Persian Gulf came copper and tin, and from the faraway Indian subcontinent came wood, ivory, and carnelian.

Not long after 3500 B.C., Sumer invented the wheel, a revolutionary improvement over the sledge and travois. With the wheel, man or beast could haul five times as much weight as without it.

Ur, Eridu, Uruk, Lagash, Nippur, Kish—so were named some of the Sumerian urban centers. Each was surrounded by a web of irrigation channels. Intensive irrigation farming could pile up crop surpluses, and these in turn could free people for pursuits other than tending fields and livestock. The layout of a Sumerian city reflected such pursuits. At its heart stood the central shrine, the temple of the main city god, its walls freshly painted white or red, in some cases adorned with mosaics of colored clay cones driven into mud walls. Nearby stood government buildings and spacious homes, interspersed with the quarters of craftsmen and the crowded, twisted alleys of the poorer people.

In one of these cities, Uruk, archaeologists have found the earliest inscribed writing, recorded on clay tablets around 3200 B.C. Scholars believe the language of the tablets is Sumerian, a language similar in grammatical structure to Turkish and Hungarian but otherwise unrelated to them. Much has been written about where the Sumerian people may have originated, but no one knows.

Some of the characters on early tablets are recognizable pictures—birds, chariots, fish. But many of the signs consist merely of abstract shapes, various kinds of circles, cones, and rods. The conventional understanding is that writing began with recognizable pictures. But an intriguing theory developed by Denise Schmandt-Besserat, associate professor of Middle Eastern studies at the University of Texas at Austin, suggests that abstract shapes came first.

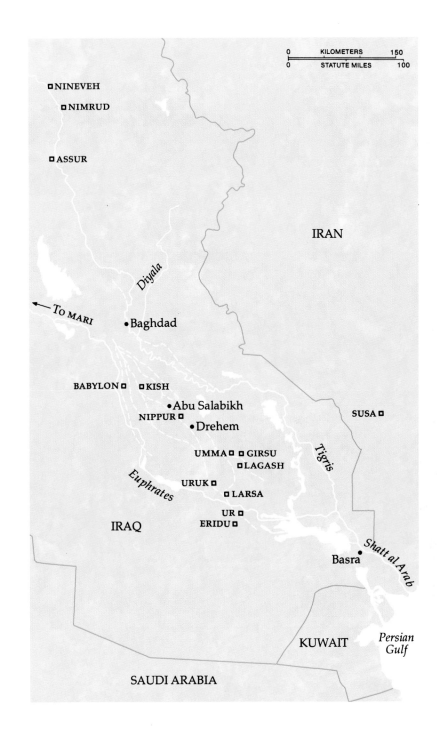

Cities of Mesopotamia rose along ancient braids of the Euphrates River (broken lines)—their probable courses inferred from old texts and modern surveys. Control of waterways created tension, then as now. An Iraq-Iran dispute over the Shatt al Arab flamed into war in 1980.

"Shrine Ur, may you rise heaven high."
Skyward rose the triple-tiered ziggurat of the moon god Nanna in the days of Ur's Third Dynasty. Pious hands laid walls of baked brick—a luxury in a land shy of fuel. "Weep holes" and wall channels drained the man-made mountain; from three directions stairways (one visible at right) converged at the second terrace. By the 20th century only a sandy heap remained, a romp for cavalrymen. Then came Leonard Woolley to clear and explore the buried site. Now visitors climb Iraq's best-preserved ziggurat—restored with ancient brick to the second tier—to look out on the skeleton of a great Sumerian city.

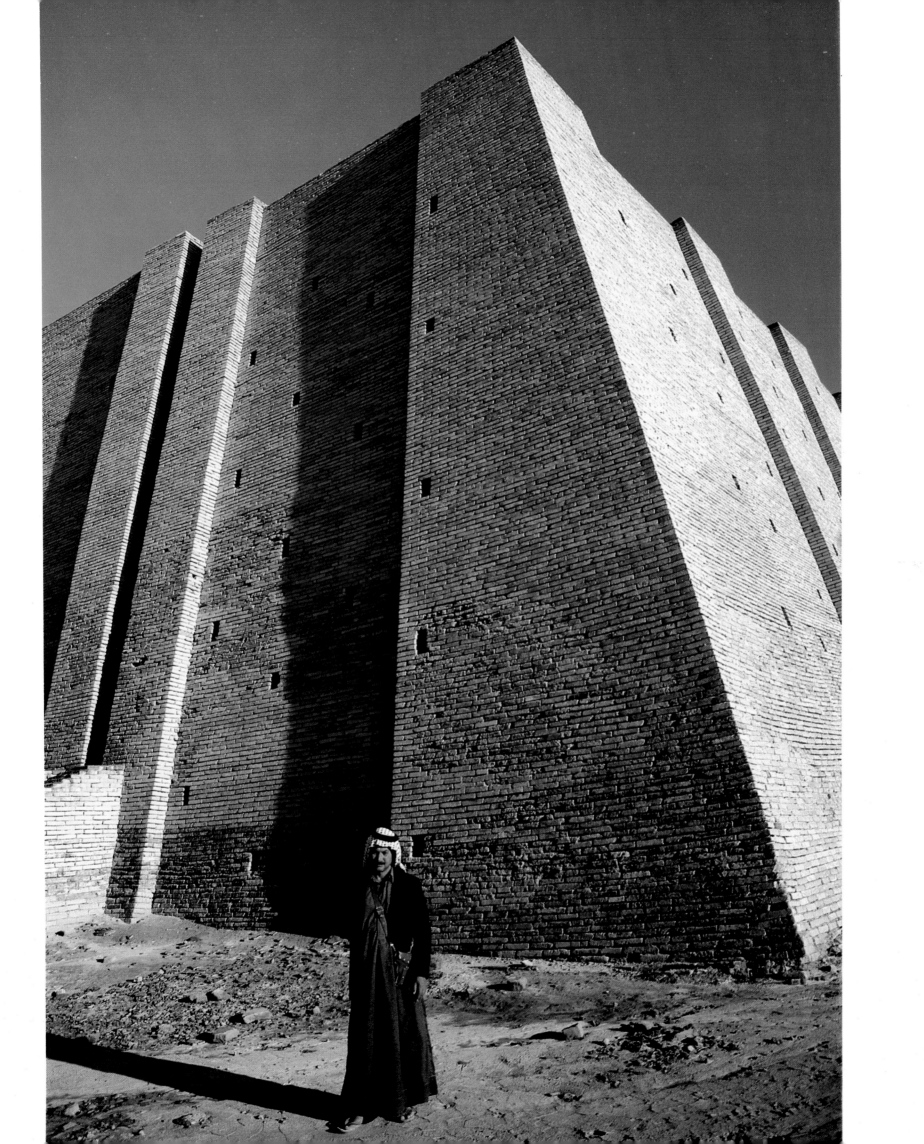

Her study sought to trace the earliest uses of clay. All across the region — from Israel to Iran — archaeologists had unearthed little clay tokens in a variety of shapes. Several looked like the abstract forms inscribed on some of the Uruk tablets, and the oldest dated from around 8000 B.C., early in the development of agriculture. Farmers would have needed some way of recording different kinds and amounts of produce. They would need records for stored goods and for bartered goods, and for herds of animals. To Professor Schmandt-Besserat, the tokens represent just such a system of recording.

For more than 4,000 years the tokens hardly vary. "Then the system starts to change dramatically around 3500 B.C.," Professor Schmandt-Besserat told me, "and there is no doubt that the changes are related to the pressures of bureaucracy in the emerging city-state." Many more kinds of tokens appear. Often they are perforated and can be strung together.

About this time came a key invention—the clay envelope. Now a trader or temple administrator could hollow a blob of clay, place tokens inside, pinch the edges together, impress his seal on the outside, and thus record a specific transaction. But, as Professor Schmandt-Besserat pointed out, the envelopes "were not transparent. If you forgot what was inside, you had to break open the envelope. So people started to impress the tokens on the surface of the envelope prior to enclosing them. One could 'read' the contents at all times."

Before long people realized they didn't need the envelope—they could do as well with a solid blob of clay, a tablet, with the marking impressed on the surface. "These crude impressions were soon replaced by more readable signs incised with a pointed stylus. These were pictures of the tokens."

Once writing with pictures was invented, she suggests, the concept could be applied to whatever

"We had a force of very wild Arab tribesmen," wrote Woolley of his start at Ur in 1922. "Moreover we were ignorant too." Four years later Woolley (front, hand on knee) had honed the crew skills needed to explore the "holocaust of treasure." Dazzling finds—royal graves with attendant ladies and charioteers and musicians buried as "tomb furniture" —drew visitors. Agatha Christie came out (via the Orient Express to Baghdad): "I fell in love with Ur, with its beauty in the evenings, the ziggurat standing up, faintly shadowed." Here she met archaeologist Max Mallowan, whom she married. With a technique using hot wax and muslin, Woolley ingeniously lifted from the soil such prizes as the crushed headdress of Queen Puabi (left), named on the cylinder seal nearby, and the "Ram Caught in a Thicket" (far left and page 47).

After delicate reconstruction these splendors of the past gleam once again. All emerged from the "great death pit" where 74 human skeletons lay. Fleece of shell and skin of gold and silver covered the rampant wooden billy goat. The piece, probably an offering stand, recalled to Woolley the thicket-trapped ram that Abraham sacrificed in place of Isaac. A lady's headdress, much like the queen's, interwove ribbons, disks, leaves, and flowers of gold; beneath hung heavy earrings, and necklaces of gold, lapis lazuli, and carnelian. A gilded bull's head with lapis beard adorned a lyre. The victims entombed with their masters evidently had music to the last; one player lay with fingers spread over the strings. Woolley dug to "get history, not to fill museum cases." His 12 years at Ur enriched both history and the museum cases in London, Baghdad, and Philadelphia.

HEADDRESS AND GOAT SHOWN ABOUT HALF ACTUAL SIZE;
HEIGHT OF LYRE DETAIL APPROXIMATELY 25 INCHES

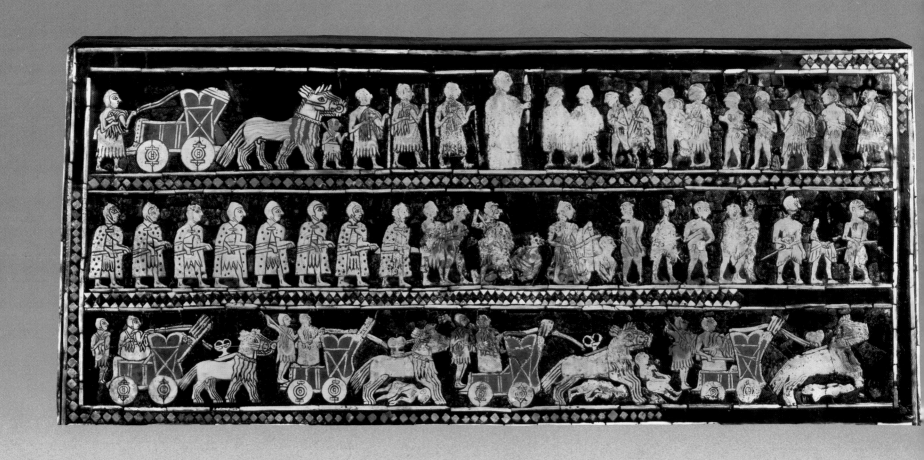

All the king's horses and all the king's men lay in pieces—but Woolley put them together again. His famed Standard of Ur, a mosaic of shell and lapis lazuli, depicts war and victory: a triumphal banquet on one side (opposite); onager-drawn chariots, soldiers, and captives humbled before the king on the other. The fluted gold cup lay near Queen Puabi.

people wanted to convey. They could scribe representations of such things as animals or parts of the human body. They could combine signs of nouns, for instance "head" and "water," to form a verb, "to drink." Whereas the tokens had been restricted to staple goods, pictography extended communication to all topics of human endeavor. The signs and their combinations came to represent not merely the original objects or related actions but also ideas and, more and more, sounds. Thus, in such a system, the character for "eye" (to borrow an example from English)

might stand for the eye itself, or it might express the idea of seeing, or it might mean the sound of "i."

The pointed stylus gave way to the wedge-shaped reed stylus, which enabled the scribe to make a variety of strokes without changing his grip. Gradually the signs became more and more schematic, until the original pictures were barely recognizable and the cuneiform characters formed a systematic script.

"The invention of writing changed the whole condition of existence," said Dr. Thorkild Jacobsen, formerly director of Chicago's Oriental Institute and later professor of Assyriology at Harvard. A hypnotic story-teller, Jacobsen has explored the mounds, the texts, and the spirit of Mesopotamia for more than half a century. He has threaded the marshes by boat, tasted the sand in blinding storms, and known the sweet slumber of balmy desert nights under a starry heaven.

"If you live in a literate society," he told me one day at Ann Arbor, Michigan, where he was serving as a visiting scholar, "you have the texts of what all the previous generations thought and felt—an unbelievable number of facts and observations."

But writing can charm and delight as well as inform us. One important belief in Sumer held that a sacred ritual marriage between the ruler and Inanna, goddess of love and fertility, brought rich harvests. The poets made the most of it. In one delightful bit of byplay, Inanna is playing hard to get, worrying about what Mama will say. Her lover Dumuzi—a shepherd king, the Tammuz of the Bible—makes up a little story for her to tell:

Inanna, most deceitful of women, let me inform you,
Say my girl friend took me with her to the public square,
*   There she entertained me with music and dancing . . . .*
Thus deceitfully stand up to your mother,
*   While we by the moonlight indulge our passion.*

The poem, said Jacobsen, was found on a school tablet in a house in Nippur, dating from around 1800

"Fill your belly—day and night make merry, let every day be full of joy, dance and make music." Death awaits us all, enjoy the moment, urges a popular epic poem. Sumerians pay heed in this festive scene employing luxurious articles like those found in the royal graves at Ur. Players pluck lyre and harp; a singer claps time. A guest drinks beer through a golden tube; servants in the rear shoulder in another jugful. Women and men alike sport earrings and necklaces; the hostess wears a gleaming headdress and beaded cloak. Feasts also accompanied temple ritual. Feasting scenes appeared on plaques (above). An inscribed peg through the pierced center would nail the relief to a temple wall, possibly to commemorate a banquet donated by a grateful worshiper. Of Enlil's temple at Nippur, a poet hymned: "Its feasts flow with fat and milk . . . Its storehouses bring . . . rejoicing."

B.C. The tablet probably came there, he explained, in the course of a remodeling job to raise the house floor —a recurring chore that continues to this day. Trash and ashes pile up outdoors, raising the street level above the house floors; then torrential rains run down the streets and flood the houses. The usual remedy is to knock in the old mud walls to raise the floor level, and build new walls. When the ancients needed more fill, said Jacobsen, they fetched discarded student exercises from nearby school dumps.

"We find all these marvelous school texts — prayers, hymns, diplomatic letters, love songs," smiled Jacobsen. "I have picked up many, many of them from the floors of ancient houses."

University of Pennsylvania excavators found the what-do-I-tell-Mama tablet in the 1890s. Professor Hermann Hilprecht, one of the leaders of the dig, bequeathed it to the University of Jena in what is now the German Democratic Republic. And there, concluded Jacobsen, "Sam Kramer found it in the 1950s." Found it and translated it for the first time.

"It was Sam Kramer, really, who discovered the Sumerian literature," said Åke Sjöberg as we talked at the University of Pennsylvania where he holds the chair once occupied by Hilprecht and later by Kramer. "He started in the 1930s, and he made fantastic discoveries. We have all depended on them."

D r. Samuel Noah Kramer has ranged the earth to study, copy, and translate cuneiform texts. A generation ago he became, in a sense, the *ummia* of us all with his book *History Begins at Sumer.* It describes 27 Sumerian firsts in such fields as government, law, ethics, literature, medicine, and agriculture.

Now there are more. He told me about them in his old office and as I strolled the Philadelphia campus beside him, a gray eminence in herringbone topcoat and navy knit watch cap, forever praising the Sumerians. He has, in recent years, discerned 12 new firsts and woven them into a revised edition of his *History* prepared for the University of Pennsylvania Press.

He had found in Sumer the first "sick society," plagued by discordant generation gaps and by rampant war amid protestations of peace. His manuscript offers the first lullaby, with a mother's soothing rockabye sounds: "oo-a a-oo-a . . . Come sleep, come sleep, Come to where my son is." The new firsts include liturgic lamentation—the form familiar to us from the Bible's Book of Lamentations—and the use of literary imagery, especially of simile. Such imagery packs vividness into a famous lament for Sumer and Ur: "The country's blood now filled its holes like metal in a mold; Bodies dissolved like fat left in the sun."

Among the tens of thousands of tablets available to scholars, scarcely one (Continued on page 56)

*O*n mirror-calm waters a boat glides by an islet crammed with livestock, reflecting a way of life Sumer knew. "He built a reed platform on the surface"—a Mesopotamian god, says one epic, began to form the world in this way. In spongy southern Iraq the Marsh Arabs, also called Madan, fence in swamps and build platforms of reed, mat, and mud, adding more as the homemade islands settle. Thin dough goes into an oven near a reed house (opposite); today's diet, as in ancient times, includes unleavened bread. A similar house (right) adorns a stone trough carved 5,000 years ago.

TROUGH DETAIL ABOUT 6 BY 12 INCHES

*T*o build a marsh house: Bind tapering bundles of towering qasab reed, and stick them in the ground, tips angled out. Bend the tips and splice together, to form parallel arches. Lay thin reed bundles across the arches as stringers. Sew on overlapping split-reed mats for siding. Move in.

Large mudhifs—*guesthouses*—*with pillared, latticed facades spread welcome mats in the marsh settlements. Here the men gather every morning to sip bitter coffee or tea and swap news. One reed house, according to the Epic of Gilgamesh, helped save mankind. A noisy, ever-multiplying humanity kept a mighty god awake; he decided to drown it. Another deity, loath to lose such a prime source of labor and devotion, let out the plan: He warned one man to tear down his reed house and from it build a boat. The man did so, loaded on his family and all kinds of animals, and rode out the fierce deluge—a Mesopotamian forerunner of Noah's biblical adventure.*

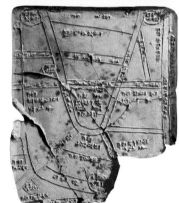

In an arid land, irrigation slaked the dry soil; but digging canals like those that vein fields of Nippur on a clay map (right) meant torturous toil. The gods of Sumer rebelled at such drudgery —and invented man to dig and tend. Man, in turn, created labor-saving technology. At Girsu (above), a weir pinched the river's flow and spewed the waters to thirsty fields. At modern-day Hit the Euphrates current spins waterwheels; jars on the rims fill, then empty, greening the gardens nearby— a technique practiced by ancient farmers. Date palms, still a staple in Iraq, prospered in Sumerian times—offering a rich, sweet food, fiber for rope, and light wood and leaves for building materials.

hints at the tale of splendor and mass human sacrifice displayed at Pennsylvania's University Museum. There I gazed upon the golden vessels and jewelry, toiletries and unguents, a goat shaped of gold and silver and lapis lazuli—all unearthed by Sir Leonard Woolley in the 1920s in the Royal Tombs at Ur, which he identified with the biblical Ur of the Chaldees. With this rich trove were the bones of soldiers and courtiers, apparently poisoned and buried with their masters and mistresses.

In Sumer's early days the city-states, it seems, elected temporary "kings" as war leaders. Eventually the kings became permanent, acquiring large retinues and great wealth. At times much fighting went on between the cities. The warring became dominant in the period called Early Dynastic, which lasted some 500 years. Woolley's sensational finds date from late in the period, around 2500 B.C.

A golden drinking tube about a yard long caught my eye. What did they drink with it? "Beer," replied Åke Sjöberg. "They had big jars, and they would stand around and drink out of the jars with these giant 'straws.' The texts tell us they were drunk sometimes, in fact, very drunk." Priests may have imbibed at cult rites. Indeed, the statues of squat, fleece-skirted temple bureaucrats often show an impressive swell around the middle. If the sculpture mirrors life, it would be no surprise. A poet composed a hymn to the beer goddess, Ninkasi, for concocting the brew that "makes the liver happy, fills the heart with joy."

Each city had its main god or goddess who dwelt in a temple. The deity's image was fed, clothed, and anointed daily. It enjoyed music with its meals, sometimes went hunting in its game park, and entertained visiting gods from out of town.

The city ruler had priestly duties; among his many burdens was that of discerning the divine will. Gudea, ruler of Lagash, dreamed that the god Ningirsu wanted a new temple. Gudea checked with a dream interpreter, then rechecked by reading the liver of a freshly slaughtered kid. Divination was part of the fabric of life; scribes compiled numerous how-to tablets. The favored method was reading sheep or goat entrails. But not everyone in need of prophetic guidance, writes Professor William W. Hallo of Yale, could afford to kill a sheep. Cheaper techniques evolved: studying the patterns of oil on water, or the patterns of smoke rising; or reading omens in dice or lots, or in arrows thrown onto the ground.

The temple owned a large share of city real estate and farmland, and might employ more than a thousand people—plowmen and herders, freshwater fishermen, brackish-water fishermen, sea fishermen, warehousemen, carpenters and smiths, teamsters,

brewers, butchers, traders, female spinners and weavers, even a chief snake charmer.

And who kept track of all this? Wool scribes, flour scribes, cattle scribes—an army of bureaucratic beavers wedging every tiny detail into the damp tablets, generating clay, so to speak, in mountainous heaps.

Nippur enjoyed the good fortune of having for its city god Enlil, the supreme god of Sumer. Just after 2100 B.C., during the renaissance of Sumerian power that became known as the Third Dynasty of Ur, King Shulgi established a receiving and records center. It stood near holy Nippur, at the modern site of Drehem. In one year the bookkeepers logged in some 28,000 cattle and 350,000 sheep.

Nippur usually stood above the battles that ravaged Sumer. Rulers of other cities contributed to the upkeep of Enlil's ziggurat shrine and built dozens of other temples as well. Over time they raised a stack of ten temples to Inanna, each built atop the ruins of the one below. Late in the sequence there appeared a new design—more spacious, more formal than the earlier ones. Shulgi built that temple and, as Sumer's rulers were wont to do, had little statues of himself placed in the foundations. The statues have been retrieved. In Chicago's superb Oriental Institute Museum I saw a green-crusted Shulgi, bearing a pan of mortar on his head in exactly the manner still practiced among workmen in the Iraq countryside.

The mound of Nippur rises more than five stories high and spreads nearly a mile across. "It's a great whale of a site," said Dr. McGuire Gibson, professor of Mesopotamian archaeology at Chicago. The enormous hump, rising into view on the road from Baghdad, is a familiar sight to him; since 1972 he has headed the institute's excavations at the holy city.

How would Nippur appear to a traveler of Shulgi's day? Although Nippur has been explored for nearly a century and has yielded 80 percent of the extant Sumerian literature, archaeology and archive

Desert shepherd grazes a flock along borderlands where nomads roamed the western flanks of Sumer. Urbanites ridiculed such wanderers "who know no house . . . the boors of the mountains," but often hired them as herders. Livestock amulets brought good luck, perhaps. Live sheep brought good income to Sumer's textile makers and exporters.

PAGES 60-61: *Gifts for the sky god Anu pour in—wriggling mallards, a choice vase, a packload of lapis lazuli, carp, fat-tailed sheep. Scribes of Anu's lovely White Temple keep a tablet tally while Uruk's ruler, with arms folded, watches carefully. The city must please its patron god. How else can it thrive? Or the vast temple staff subsist? A product of the newly invented potter's wheel sits by the basket of dates in this scene of about 3200 B.C.*

paint a patchwork picture, and conjecture must play a part. Still, Dr. Gibson was willing to have a go.

"You would see a city surrounded by a wall some 3½ yards high, nearly two miles around. Outside the walls there are little corrals with animals, and people cooking near them. Villagers or nomads who had come to Nippur, to trade perhaps. If you were coming from the south, you might come in at the gate called the 'Uruk Gate' on the ancient map of Nippur.

"Now, compared to the outside, the streets are narrow, cool, and dark. But it's a mud-brick town. There's some dust around. After passing through a residential area in the lower town, you'd climb the mound, maybe stop and buy some bread to munch on, a flat bread like pita. There's a bakery there. Five or six ovens are turning out maybe 1,500 loaves a day. We've found one receipt, from a later time, for bread and sheep tongues ordered for workers.

"You could, by boat or bridge of boats, cross a canal to the eastern part of the city, where they might be building Shulgi's Inanna Temple. They'd have a pit, in which they put straw, water, and soil, and then they'd jump up and down and walk around in it to mix mortar. They'd carry it in pans on their heads, just as the Shulgi statue does. The bricks are already made. These are superb, fired bricks—very little salt in the clay, no trash, no sherds.

"You might move on to the outer walls of the ziggurat, which is nearby. Shulgi's father Ur-Nammu built it, and it looks magnificent, standing above everything in the city, with its temple on top. There's also a kind of temple off to the side on the ground level, a food preparation place. Here the offerings are made ready; then they're taken to the temple on top. But we don't know whether any ordinary people ever got inside the ziggurat walls to see the ritual."

South of the ziggurat lies the site known as Tablet Hill, where so much of the literary legacy of Sumer has been found. It has been called a scribal quarter. That's probably a misnomer, said Gibson. "We've found tablets everywhere we've ever dug a hole at Nippur," he went on. "There were tablets everywhere, scribes everywhere." Like Foggy Bottom in Washington, D.C., Tablet Hill seems to have combined high-class housing and a government complex.

Nippur today is the haunt of wolf and hawk, says Gibson. In the early 1890s excavators had to approach by boat. In time the land went from marsh to desert to irrigated fields. Later a belt of dunes drifted in, filled archaeologists' holes, and buried farmland. Now the dunes have retreated; new canal trenches score the land. The government has wired the dig for electricity and delivers safe water by tanker truck.

But gone are the fabulous Iraqi chefs who served the British Army in World War I and then, for decades, the embassies in Baghdad and the archaeologists' field expeditions. "They were great, even in their 70s, under the most unbelievable conditions," says Gibson. There was the indelible day in 1965 when he visited the nearby dig at Abu Salabikh in the rainy season. "The dig staff lived in reed houses that leaked like crazy, and people went to sleep holding umbrellas over their heads. It was a holiday, and everything was dripping and miserable—and here came this cook from his small tent, knee-deep in mud, bringing this incredibly beautiful turkey with all the trimmings. And later on he delivered a dessert, a meringue basket, you know, with custard inside. In the awful muck, on two of these pressure stoves—two little kerosene burners!"

Another virtuoso performed wonders at the stoves in the 1960s. Dr. Robert D. Biggs, professor of Assyriology at Chicago, was responsible for the tablets excavated at Abu Salabikh. They came out extremely fragile, cracked and full of worm holes. Biggs spent four months baking them in homemade kilns at nearby Nippur. Then he studied them, made drawings of them, and, nearly a decade later, published them.

Dating from around 2500 B.C., they comprise an extraordinary trove—some are familiar literary compositions, but produced about 800 years earlier than most of the known Sumerian literary works. "I think it's terribly important," Biggs told me in Chicago, "that writing, even at that early time, was used not just to keep accounts. By the period of these texts they're using the system for writing literature, which implies a concern with things other than the necessities of daily life. People took pleasure in a nice story. There was a certain sense of art for art's sake."

Biggs discovered that about half the scribes who signed the tablets had Semitic names. Semitic people of that time, he said, "have generally been pictured as nomads herding sheep and goats. It's quite a different picture to find them in a city writing Sumerian texts at a center of learning."

With the conquest of Sumer by Sargon the Great of Akkad around 2340 B.C., a Semitic dynasty took power. Royal inscriptions were written in Akkadian, the king's language. The dynasty ruled for nearly two hundred years. Its capital, Akkad or Agade, lies somewhere to the north of Sumer; no one has pinpointed the site. A poem entitled "The Curse of Agade" tells us that the Akkadians defiled Enlil's shrine at Nippur. The gods vowed to obliterate Akkad for all time; their curse has held good for forty centuries, an enticing challenge to archaeology.

In a famous literary disputation, the god Enlil referees a poetic debate between the Pickax and the Plow. "I am the faithful farmer of mankind," says the Plow. "I come ahead of you," says the Pickax. "I make ditches, I make canals." Enlil awards the victory to the

Pickax. In this dry land it is really no contest. To farm in southern Mesopotamia, one must irrigate.

With oil revenues beginning to flow, Iraq's government in the late 1950s sought to settle farmers in a formerly cultivated region east of Baghdad. But after a few years the farmers began to leave the land. There was too much salt in the soil.

The threat of crop-stifling salt looms wherever heavy irrigation has been applied to flat, semiarid, poorly drained land. Farmers in the Imperial and San Joaquin Valleys of California have had to cope with it.

Facing the expense of vast drainage systems, Iraqi officials thought of their land's golden past—the web of irrigated fields, the great surpluses. Perhaps the ancients had known something modern agriculturists didn't. The government asked Thorkild Jacobsen and Robert Adams to look into it. The ancients had no secrets, Adams concluded. They were aware of the salinity in their fields, they even measured its extent; but they didn't know what to do about it.

Adams's study of settlement patterns suggests repeated cycles of growth and disintegration. The city elite tended to expand cultivation, enjoying luxury and civilized pursuits while a hard-pressed peasantry labored to provide the resources. The system was inherently unstable. With a hint of breakdown in the power structure, or the failure of a crop, peasants on the city outskirts might gather their flocks, desert the fields, and become nomads. People voted with their feet, said Adams. And centralized power in a single dynasty seldom lasted more than a few generations.

Thorkild Jacobsen studied the ancient records to gauge the impact of salt in the soil. Around 2400 B.C. the city-states of Lagash and Umma battled over a border area. Umma, lying upstream, interrupted the supply of water. Lagash parried by cutting a canal from the Tigris. The rich gush of water lured southern Sumer into over-irrigation. The briny water table rose. By 2100, crop yields declined by half; wheat cultivation was all but abandoned, replaced by the more salt-tolerant barley. "Sumerian cities dwindled to villages," writes Jacobsen. Other factors were involved, he adds, but salt unquestionably played an important part in the breakup of Sumerian civilization.

After 2000 B.C. power moved north, to the Semitic empire of Hammurabi of Babylon, in time to Assyria, then to Babylon once more. In 539 B.C. the Persians conquered Babylon, and history turned its spotlight away from the land between the rivers—where, more than 2,000 years earlier, the resourceful Sumerians had created their shining cities and their system of writing. The end, we read in the Book of Daniel, was foretold in writing: the handwriting on the wall.

Wings of lapis lazuli, head and tail of gold—the lion-headed eagle Imdugud symbolized the god who protected domestic animals. Around 2500 B.C. the King of Ur sent this amulet, with other gifts, up the Euphrates to the King of Mari, who controlled a trade route vital to Sumer. Two centuries later all Sumer and its trade routes as well lay in the grip of Semitic conquerors: Sargon of Akkad had forged the first Mesopotamian empire. A new, more lifelike sculpture came into vogue, embodied in a royal bronze head (opposite) often identified as Sargon. Later invaders hacked its eyes, ears, nose, and beard— apparently an act of political mutilation.

CICCIONE/RAPHO

LION-HEADED EAGLE APPROXIMATELY 5 INCHES HIGH, BRONZE HEAD (OPPOSITE) 12 INCHES

*S*hovel brigade heads for the shade and another day of digging into holy Nippur. The site's flat-topped dump mounds (left) rise to impressive heights before the shrunken ziggurat; at its crest, in place of a temple, stands a modern expedition house. Bedouins and their camels file by, bound for grazing ground or trading village in the timeless rounds of the nomad. At far left, below, King Ur-Nammu, founder of Sumer's last glorious dynasty, carries mud in effigy to mark his building of the ziggurat some 4,000 years ago. Excavators found the royal hod carrier, with beads and plaque, under the walls of the shrine honoring the god Enlil. Another foundation box (far left, center) bears the figure of Ur-Nammu's son Shulgi, builder of a temple to Inanna. Ur-Nammu revived Sumer's power, expanded trade and farming, and produced a code of laws — the earliest yet found.

Pushcart railroad clears drifting sand as excavators probe near the ziggurat of Nippur. Year after year the slowly moving dune belt plagued the dig with obliterating burdens; then it shifted course and began to drift away. Not far from the ziggurat, archaeologists uncovered a stack of ten temples spanning 3,000 years—all honoring Inanna, most awesome deity in Sumerian literature. "My Queen, you are all-devouring"—so reads a hymn to Inanna (below) written about 2300 B.C. by the priestess Enheduanna, history's earliest known author. One temple in the stack at Nippur stretched longer than a football field. King Shulgi built it. A poem tells how he once ran from Ur to Nippur, about a hundred miles, and dined with his divine spouse, Inanna—all in the same day.

LEFT: GEORG GERSTER; BELOW: VICTOR R. BOSWELL, JR.
TABLET APPROXIMATELY 5 BY 8 INCHES

*Pure, bright land, "the place where the sun rises": A paradise of Sumerian myth finds a locale in a golden morning on the lower Tigris (*PRECEDING PAGES*), as the sun climbs above wet lowlands where the marsh folk and the pelicans fish. Sumer's texts mention nearly a hundred kinds of fishes; one appears bound for a banquet table in a detail from a temple plaque (left) of*

about 2800 B.C. Local tradition places the Garden of Eden in the marshes. Some archaeologists suggest that prehistoric people, dependent upon the bounty of the wilds, would have found a paradise in marshlands teeming with fish and waterfowl. To the northwest, the rivers offered their rich silt and spring floods. When farmers learned to apportion the waters and plow the land, a fabled granary flourished on the alluvial plain of Mesopotamia. The way then stood open for Sumer's pioneering venture into literacy and the evolution of urban life.

By SEYMOUR L. FISHBEIN
Photographed by IRA BLOCK

THE ROYAL CITIES

*D*ome of the Rock, one of the earliest Islamic monuments, has graced the Jerusalem skyline since 691. The Koran recounts the story of Muhammad's night journey from Mecca to this site, where Solomon's Temple had stood. Christians, too, revere the city so closely tied to the founder of their faith. Dormition Abbey (right background) marks the traditional site of Mary's "falling asleep" at the end of her life on earth.

PAGES 72-73: Israelis crowd the Western Wall—the famed Wailing Wall, relic of a retaining wall of Herod's Temple alongside the Dome—in a yearly rite that laments the loss of the Temple. Near here Solomon triumphed over a rival who sought Israel's crown. The opponent found refuge in catching "hold on the horns" of an altar. The horned altar pictured above lay in fragments in Israelite Megiddo.

HEIGHT OF ALTAR APPROXIMATELY 16 INCHES

"How doth the city sit solitary, that was full of people! . . . She that was great among the nations and princess among the provinces, how is she become tributary! She weepeth sore in the night. . . ." Those days of Jerusalem's agony lie 2,500 years in the past, yet she has not forgotten. This night the city is full of people, and she weepeth sore, remembering. The people come streaming in with the evening breeze, the benediction that redeems each acrid summer day. They pour through soot-stained gates of golden stone into Jerusalem's sacred heart: the Old City, with its pulsing bazaars, and shrines that remember the mission of Jesus, and Islam's glorious beacon—the Dome of the Rock—that soon or late rivets every eye.

Below one side of this exquisite shrine run the weathered limestone courses of the Western, or Wailing, Wall. Here, like filings to a magnet, the streams of Jews converge. Many wear soft shoes or go barefoot, as mourners do, and sit on the stone floor; for eventide has brought the ninth day in the Hebrew month of Av. Around this date, near this spot, Babylonians sacked the Temple built by King Solomon. Around this date Roman legions razed the shrine known as the Second Temple. So the ninth of Av became a night and day of fasting and ritual mourning, its dirges tolling the catastrophes of Jewish history. Beside the floodlighted wall we begin with the Book of Lamentations, the Hebrew elegies recalling when Jerusalem—"she that was great among the nations"—fell to Nebuchadnezzar of Babylon in 586 B.C. (or, in Jewish custom, B.C.E., Before the Common Era).

She had reached her zenith among the nations some four centuries earlier, when David and Solomon ruled a united Israel for most of the tenth century B.C. The story comes to us in the Old Testament books of Samuel, Kings, and Chronicles, building to the golden age when Solomon "exceeded all the kings of the earth for riches and for wisdom."

How much is history, how much the embellishment of a people in crisis striving to retrieve that soaring moment of divine favor? Archaeology and history pursue a faint, often obliterated trail into those days of the Bible. At times the path doubles back. A generation ago we thought we had found King Solomon's mines, his stables, and his Red Sea port. Now, with new knowledge, they have joined that vast realm of

Under the Dome lies the sacred rock, Sakhrah, regarded by Muslims as the point from which Muhammad ascended to heaven. Upon this rock also, tradition says, Abraham prepared to sacrifice Isaac. When Crusaders held the city, they turned the Dome into a church; a religious order here took the name Poor Knights of Christ and of the Temple of Solomon—the Knights Templars.

issues for which Israeli scholars have an all-purpose label: *"pruhblemmahteecal."*

Before Solomon, the nomadic, warring Israelite tribes could leave only meager clues of a material culture. With Solomon's fabulous reign, archaeology probes for the kind of monuments left by other rich ancient cultures. Though excavators have yet to discover the gilded splendor described in the Bible, they have found monumental remains of Solomon's royal cities. And historians sense his presence in his time—a merchant prince, a diplomat of skill and practical wisdom. The trail beckons, and the quest for the buried past goes on, in this land where past times are a pastime. From earth's far corners, thousands each year join the quest, to dig as volunteers, to study, or—as I did for a few midsummer weeks—simply to observe and seek understanding.

The trail now leads me several hundred yards south of the Western Wall, outside the Old City's Dung Gate. Here, Dr. Yigal Shiloh of the Hebrew University of Jerusalem is riding the hottest dig in Israel, with an international cast of hundreds, including the California teacher whom he greets on his early rounds:

"Good morning America!"

"Good morning, Israel."

"Professor, do you think we can get masks?" yells another volunteer out of a dust billow. "And guns?" Shiloh asks, gently needling this little enclave from the land of the Wild, Wild West. This is the site called the City of David, perched on a steep hillside above the Kidron Valley. Nowhere does this tilted jumble resemble a textbook tell, one of those neat horizontal mounds in which layers of occupation descend logically from latest on top to earliest at bottom.

The Roman layer, say, from the time of Christ, would lie above Hellenistic levels of the preceding centuries; and these in turn would lie higher than the Iron Age remains that coincide with the centuries of the Israelite kingdoms. Lower still would rest Bronze Age artifacts of the Canaanites. But on a hillside, early occupants may build high up, later ones lower down. "Here," explained David Tarler as we sorted out the section he supervises, "we're standing on top of a fortification from the second century B.C., and we're looking *up* at remains from the Iron Age which ended in 586 B.C."

Here stood the stronghold King David conquered about 1000 B.C. from the Canaanite people called Jebusites. Commanding a strategic crossing on the mountain backbone of the land, it offered an excellent vantage for ruling the northern and southern tribes that had coalesced under the warrior chieftain into the single nation of Israel. Amid the piles of debris emerge the lines of stone walls, standing pillars of houses, hard-packed floors. Across the Kidron Valley the Arab village of Silwan climbs the eastern slope, cubes and

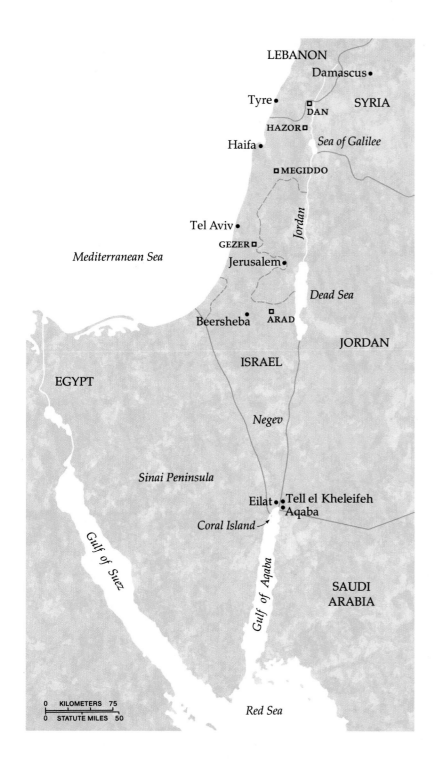

rectangles set on filled terraces. Ancient Jerusalem looked much the same, remarks Dr. Shiloh.

Sunlight wilts the morning; workers at the dig reach for water, as surely as workers in the city did in biblical days. Water determined the site. The city required a defensible height, but also an all-season water supply—a source for the rainless months from April to November that would be accessible in time of siege. The one source that fit the need flows in the valley below the City of David. It is the Spring Gihon, also known as the Virgin's Spring (Mary is said to have washed the clothes of Jesus here). Gihon in Hebrew means "gusher"; the spring still gushes today. The ancients hacked tunnels through bedrock to keep the water within reach while denying it to attackers.

Solomon was crowned at the Spring Gihon 3,000 years ago. As David grew old, the First Book of Kings records, his son Adonijah plotted for the throne. Bathsheba, mother of Solomon but not of Adonijah, appealed to David. He ordered Solomon ridden "upon mine own mule" to Gihon and there anointed. "And they blew the trumpet; and all the people said, God save king Solomon." A quarter of a mile away, at Ein Rogel, Adonijah heard the commotion, then learned the disastrous news. Adonijah "feared because of Solomon . . . and went and caught hold on the horns of the altar." Such sacred altars gave refuge to those charged with crime. Horned altars have been found in biblical cities; one stands in Jerusalem's Israel Museum. A small park with climbing bars and slides marks the site of Ein Rogel today.

The sound that signaled Adonijah's downfall— the blast of the trumpet, or ram's horn — echoes through the ages. In the month of Elul, which follows Av, the ram's horn—*shofar* in Hebrew—sounds daily in Jerusalem, heralding the High Holy Days, the Hebrew New Year and the Day of Atonement. The shofar punctuates Old Testament history. It was heard on Sinai, in the conquests of Joshua, at the arrival of the Ark of the Covenant in Jerusalem. It marked the years of jubilee, proclaiming "liberty throughout the land"— the phrase from Leviticus that appears on America's Liberty Bell.

After a reign of forty years, David "slept with his fathers." Solomon had ruled jointly; now he ruled alone, a very different personality from his father. Professor David Noel Freedman of the University of Michigan has tautly sketched the contrast between the two: "David was a warrior, Solomon a diplomat; David a lover, Solomon a luster; David a poet, Solomon a phrase-maker." Solomon was also the great builder. We read in 1 Kings 9:15: "And this is the reason of the levy which king Solomon raised; for to build the house of the Lord, and his own house . . . and the wall of Jerusalem, and Hazor, and Megiddo, and Gezer."

Of the "house of the Lord," the Temple, Professor

Solomon's biblical Israel commanded trade routes between Syria and Mesopotamia to the northeast and Egypt to the southwest. An alliance with Phoenicia on the northern coast gave Israel access to skilled craftsmen and merchant mariners. Together the allies ventured forth on sea trade from the southern biblical port of Ezion-geber, perhaps located in the vicinity of Aqaba. Archaeologists have unearthed Solomon's fortifications in the strategic, multilayered cities of Gezer, Megiddo, and Hazor. On the slopes of Jerusalem the search goes on for relics of Israel's ancient royal capital.

Freedman writes: "Solomon's greatest monument, of bronze, wood, and stone, charms and puzzles readers, and challenges the precision of scholars." The Bible offers much detail, yet no clear picture. Other works mentioned in 1 Kings 9:15 stand in sharper light, thanks in good part to the masterful field campaigns and intuitive flare of Dr. Yigael Yadin.

The son of the late Professor E. L. Sukenik, he had grown up with archaeology. In Israel's battle for statehood in the 1940s, he served as chief of operations in the defense forces under the code name Yadin, which he adopted as his own.

He went to Hazor in 1955. "Why? Was it because of 1 Kings 9?" I asked him at his home in Jerusalem. A quarter of a century had passed; he now served as deputy prime minister of a troubled Israel. Yet he answered without pause. The memory was fresh. Archaeological talk seemed a pleasurable interlude.

"I went because it was the largest mound in the country," he began. "Second, the whole northern part of the country, archaeologically speaking, was terra incognita for the Old Testament. And third, because of the biblical connotations." Joshua had conquered Hazor, and Solomon had built there. Although Solomon enjoyed a generally peaceful reign, he would want fortified cities along strategic routes of his trading empire, Yadin observed. Gezer, Megiddo, and Hazor would qualify. Gezer, just off the modern Jerusalem–Tel Aviv superhighway, overlooked the ancient coastal plain road between Egypt and the north, and also the spur to Jerusalem. To the north the coastal road forked through a pass in the Carmel Ridge. At the far opening stood Megiddo, commanding not only the traffic to Galilee and Damascus but also the rich Jezreel Valley granary. Solomon's grain earned much Phoenician cedar, cypress, and gold. Armies have fought for Megiddo from the fourth millennium B.C. to World War I; the Book of Revelation envisions it as the site of the final battle yet to come—Armageddon.

To the northeast, nine miles beyond the Sea of Galilee, the mound of Hazor rose above the fruitful Jordan Valley; here roads forked eastward toward Damascus and north toward Lebanon and Anatolia. And here in the 1950s Yadin uncovered 21 levels of occupation. Some of the earlier Canaanite cities sprawled over 200 acres. Solomon's city covered less than 10. "I knew I was slowly approaching it step by step," Yadin recalled. "I believed in that verse in the Bible." So much so that when he neared the "clincher," a distinctive city gate that would confirm what pottery and the relative level of the city already implied, he traced its fortifications out on the ground as a prophecy of what his workers would find.

A generation earlier the University of Chicago excavation at Megiddo had unearthed a Solomonic level; its gate had a tower and three chambers flanking each side of the passage. The Bible linked Solomonic Megiddo and Hazor in the same verse. Yadin reasoned that a royal fortification program would use the same architect and same design for all the cities included.

Out of the mound of Hazor emerged the foundation of a gate with a tower and three chambers flanking each side of the entryway. Pious Jewish diggers saw it take shape in amazement—until they heard the Bible had played a part in guiding Yadin. The gate structure's dimensions—some 60 feet wide, tower to tower, with a 14-foot-wide passageway 66 feet long—mirrored those at Megiddo almost exactly.

The fortifications included walls, but here Yadin's reasoning seemed flawed. Solomon had enclosed Hazor with a casemate wall, a double wall with dividers, forming a long string of rooms with openings into the city. At Megiddo the earlier excavators had linked the gate to a solid wall. Casemates were cheaper to build and offered extra space. They couldn't take as much pounding as a solid wall, yet Yadin felt they were adequate in Solomon's day. Not until the appearance of mightier "breaching machines," the Assyrian battering rams of a century later, did Israel's defenders respond with massive, solid walls.

Yadin decided to have a look at Megiddo. In a series of short probes there, he found the casemate design he had expected; it ran *under* the solid wall. Sadly, the city level with the solid wall included what had become known around the world as King Solomon's stables—long, pillared structures with recessed stone troughs. The stables are later—of King Ahab's reign in the 9th century B.C., perhaps. "I destroyed a myth," Yadin recalled. "It's a pity, but that's the truth." Other scholars, though not Yadin, insist the buildings are not even stables but rather storage buildings, the troughs perhaps used to feed pack animals while they were being unloaded. Some archaeologists have also rejected Yadin's basic view of a single, unique design in Solomon's city fortification. Yadin and his supporters have held firm. Yet his own work proves that each new turn of the spade may undermine entrenched conclusions.

As for Solomon's Gezer, declared a smiling Yadin, it was "the greatest discovery I ever made without excavating." The discovery lay buried in the report of an early 20th-century dig at Gezer—a sketch of a casemate wall linked to a three-chambered structure. It was labeled "Maccabean Castle." The Maccabees ruled Palestine eight centuries after Solomon. Yadin had seen the sketch hundreds of times; after Hazor, it struck him that the "castle" was half of a Solomonic gate. A Hebrew Union College team, digging at Gezer in the 1960s, soon found the missing half.

The Megiddo and Gezer gates revealed identical

Tanned bodies, bleached stones: summer in the City of David. Diggers clear a steep pitch where Israelites crafted a unified city plan —terraced houses, a drainage system for rainy-season runoff. In the eighth century B.C. the city resembled modern-day Silwan across the Kidron Valley. The site includes a monumental stone wall that may date from the tenth-century heyday of David and Solomon. Within the hill Keith Monteith (below) ascends Warren's Shaft, which he helped to clear. Loose fill still buries the steps leading to waters of the Spring Gihon—a vital link in ancient times of siege. When the going gets too steep for machines, the load falls on the Jerusalem donkey, time-tested performer in these storied hills.

masonry techniques, using rectangles of dressed limestone called ashlars. Israelites usually built with unhewn fieldstones; costly dressed stone reflected regal tastes in a flourishing realm.

City gates and their environs made handy multipurpose areas—courthouse, market, political forum. Dr. Ze'ev Herzog of Tel Aviv University, who has studied ancient gates, told me that multiple use could evolve easily as years, even decades passed without a military threat. The Bible records a variety of activities. Deuteronomy cites the gate as a place of punishment. The Book of Ruth tells of Boaz negotiating with elders at the gate of Bethlehem for the hand of Ruth.

King David's rebellious son, Absalom, seeking supporters, reminds me for all the world of a modern politician working factory gates: "And Absalom rose up early and stood beside the way of the gate. . . . When any man came nigh to him to do him obeisance, he put forth his hand, and took him, and kissed him. . . . So Absalom stole the hearts of the men of Israel." But in vain. Absalom lost his cause and his life.

Gezer is a lonely, untended tell. Not so Hazor and Megiddo; both are national parks. At both, visitors trace the old walls, the remains of palaces and sanctuaries, the stone feeding troughs, the laboriously engineered water systems of the ninth century B.C. Museum exhibits and guidebooks and signposts offer welcome aids to flesh these skeletons of splendor.

Far to the south of the breezy heights of Megiddo and Hazor, Israel invites us to another biblical national park, the reconstructed citadel of Arad. Here we walk the ramparts, looking down on a huge, much earlier Canaanite city and on Bedouins and their flocks undulating along the suede hills of the Negev desert. Rabbits arc over the weeds, birds home into burrows in stone crannies, lizards beyond counting scuttle over the site. Within the citadel the late Professor Yohanan Aharoni of Tel Aviv University discovered what he interpreted as a sanctuary with a Holy of Holies; it held incense altars and a standing stone slab called a *massebah*. Some scholars, citing this find, believe there were several shrines of Yahweh outside of Jerusalem.

Southwest of Arad the tell of Beersheba bulges up near the growing industrial city of the same name. When Solomon organized his empire, enjoying tribute from vassal kings, his people "dwelt safely, every man under his vine and under his fig tree, from Dan even to Beersheba, all the days of Solomon."

"She layeth her hands to the spindle." As in the Book of Proverbs, women spin and weave in an open-sided room; in the central court, others shape dough and bake it. The court, two flanking rooms, and one broad rear room (at far left) make up the typical four-room house that sheltered Israelites of Solomon's day and for centuries after.

Beersheba, according to its excavator, Professor Aharoni, is the "clearest case yet discovered" of a biblical store city. Its original design goes back to the tenth century B.C. The complex plan includes a ring road paralleling the city wall, with houses set radially on the road. There were lateral streets, government buildings, storehouses. Dwellings at Beersheba include examples of the famous four-room house, ancient Israel's tract house. The pattern— a central room or courtyard open to the street, with two long, pillared side rooms and a broad rear room—has been found in Hazor, Jerusalem, and elsewhere in Israel, dating from around 1200 B.C. to the Babylonian conquest six centuries later. The basic plan could be adapted for stables, storehouses, or barracks. In some places stone stairways suggest two-story buildings.

A model four-room house stands open for inspection at Tel Aviv's Museum Haaretz, inviting us into the domestic life of the people of the Old Testament. Round clay oven for baking and stone fireplace for cooking stand in the open courtyard. One side room contains a spindle for spinning wool and flax, and a vertical loom with its doughnut-shaped loom weights. The other side room holds kitchenware: narrow-necked jars for oil and wine; wide jars for grain; dipping juglets and spice mills; rough, sloping stones for grinding grain. The narrow back room that spans the other three has been fitted out as a sleeping, living, and dining room.

The annual lament of the ninth of Av ends a three-week period of mourning. During those weeks no Jewish wedding takes place in Israel. On the tenth day of Av, at Moshav Bareqet, some 13 miles from Tel Aviv, preparations for the wedding of Esther Matuf to her second cousin Moshe Matuf begin immediately. And no wonder. Pre-nuptial ceremonies alone will last a full week, a different one each day. There will be the formal betrothal, with the anointing of Esther. There will be the exchange of gifts by the two families, with mock complaints over the size of the gifts. There will be the braiding of Esther's hair to symbolize her passage from girlhood to womanhood. And on and on until the wedding. And more after that.

Esther's people thus keep alive the folkways they brought with them some thirty years ago from their ancestral village of Habban, located in the Democratic Republic of South Yemen. There over the centuries the isolated Jewish community trained its own rabbis and rigidly kept the faith. The Habbani men crafted silver wares, loading supplies on their backs or on camels and going off on selling trips for weeks and months.

They practiced plural marriages in the custom of Oriental Jews; their healers cured ills by searing patients with red-hot brands; they made dough with

*Ashlar masonry—neatly dressed limestone blocks—
traces Gezer's six-chambered gate, best preserved of the
three found in Solomon's cities. Gezer, where the hill
country joins the coastal plain, belonged to Egypt. The
pharaoh, says the First Book of Kings, gave it "for a
present unto his daughter, Solomon's wife."*

PRECEDING PAGES: *Parallel lines of a casemate wall arc
across Hazor in Galilee. The wall and its gate (at
right), similar to those of Gezer and Megiddo, identify
Solomon's stronghold. Twin rows of pillars remain
from a huge storehouse built a century later.*

hand-turned grindstones and baked it over open fires.
Some customs persist today; others gradually yield,
according to Dr. Laurence Loeb, a University of Utah
anthropologist who spends his summers at Bareqet.
Silver-crafting has waned. New plural marriages are
banned in Israel, and the old ones lack bliss. The men
no longer travel, and their presence at home seems to
stir tension, Dr. Loeb found. The women have taken
jobs and understandably have become more assertive.

The Habbani are a "smell-oriented culture," Loeb
told me one day at the village. In greetings, instead of
kissing, they sniff each other's hands or necks. Their
ceremonies make heavy use of incense. Their town of
Habban bestrides an old incense trade route, and some
elders trace traditions to the land of frankincense and
myrrh, the biblical land of Sheba. As the story goes,
when the Queen of Sheba ended her visit with King
Solomon, the king sent a retinue of soldiers and
settlers back with her to Sheba. Thought to be ancient
Saba in southern Arabia, Sheba may have spanned
today's Arab Republic of Yemen, or North Yemen,

along with South Yemen. From that retinue, the elders say, eventually arose the community of Habban.

Countless are the legends that grew out of the visit described in 1 Kings 10—a tale of luxury and daunting wisdom, even a hint of romance that proved enormously fecund in producing legendary descendants of Solomon and the queen. "And when the queen of Sheba heard of the fame of Solomon . . . she came to prove him with hard questions. And she came to Jerusalem with a very great train, with camels that bare spices, and very much gold, and precious stones . . . And when the queen of Sheba had seen all Solomon's wisdom, and the house that he had built, and the meat of his table, and the sitting of his servants, and the attendance of his ministers . . . there was no more spirit in her. . . . And king Solomon gave unto the queen of Sheba all her desire, whatsoever she asked. . . . So she turned and went to her own country . . . ."

Skeptics regard the account itself a legendary figment. But Dr. Gus Van Beek of the Smithsonian Institution, who has excavated in ancient Saba, told me there was good reason for the visit—albeit the queen would scarcely trek 1,400 desert miles and back to pay a social call and pose some riddles. Saba enjoyed a rich international trade in frankincense and myrrh, both valued in antiquity for use in ritual, cosmetics, and medicine. The trees that yield these aromatic resins grow only in southern Arabia and nearby Somalia.

Saba's important caravan routes ended in Solomon's domain. "Here was a 'new boy' controlling territory the caravans had to cross," said Dr. Van Beek. "I think she would have gone up there to check him out, and to make what we would call today an economic agreement." And possibly also to see about ocean trade: Solomon's Red Sea fleet — built by the Phoenician Hiram of Tyre, who had contributed so much to Solomon's monuments in Jerusalem—might require port concessions controlled by Saba.

"And king Solomon made a navy of ships in Ezion-geber, which is beside Eloth, on the shore of the Red Sea." Where is Solomon's Red Sea port? Four decades ago Dr. Nelson Glueck placed Ezion-geber at Tell el Kheleifeh in Jordan, just north of the head of the Gulf of Eilat, or Aqaba, a finger of the Red Sea. He also identified the mines at Timna, some 18 miles north, as King Solomon's mines. Later explorations indicate that Solomon's Israel dug no copper there, though modern Israel does. Tell el Kheleifeh yields evidence of a significant Israelite occupation, but there have been no finds of the burnished pottery ware that dates Solomon's reign for today's archaeologists.

On a lovely Egyptian islet in the coral-strewn waters of the gulf, at the foot of a crumbling medieval citadel, under a dehydrating desert sun that sends us to water jugs every few minutes, Uzi Avner tells me of a long shot in the search for Ezion-geber.

Avner is Israel's district archaeologist for the southern Negev. Of all the possibilities, he says, Jordan's port of Aqaba, some seven miles north of us, seems the most likely. It has the richest sources of water. Nearby Eilat, Israel's modern port, does not seem a strong bet. Tell el Kheleifeh may yet turn up solid clues. The long shot is this 300-yard-long island, which has a touristy name—Coral Island—and a more formal one, Jezirat Faraun, Island of the Pharaohs. Surface and underwater archaeology have produced no strong spoor of Ezion-geber. Yet look here. Avner strolls the shoreline, pointing to parallel rows of stones with transverse dividers—the remains of a casemate wall. A lagoon scallops the island's western shore. The lagoon's site is significant. "The prevailing wind," he explains, "is north-northeast. This can never be dangerous to ships at the head of the gulf. Since the wind comes from land, there is no chance for the waves to accumulate power. But a couple of times a year, very suddenly the north wind stops, and the air stands still for about half an hour. Then the south wind starts. It comes on thirty, forty miles an hour, a storm called *aillah* in Arabic. Now the waves have the whole length of the gulf to build up power. Not until I stood and watched them smash up on the beaches of Eilat did I realize how powerful they are.

"I've also stood here on the southwest shore during one of those storms. You can hear the wind roaring all around—but the water is calm." Such a stormproof anchorage would attract ancient seamen — though they'd have to import fresh water here. The island has none. In sum, the Coral Island has a "very high potential" as a port site in antiquity. Ezion-geber? An enchanting possibility—but problematical.

*W*here the Reverend Keith Monteith explores the Israelite past, in the rock beneath the City of David in Jerusalem, the sun's heat is no problem. In cool darkness he crouches and slides along the loose fill of the passage known as Warren's Shaft, which leads to the Spring Gihon. A major goal of the City of David dig has been to increase knowledge of the ancient underground water system. One tunnel, built by King Hezekiah around 700 B.C., snakes Gihon's waters horizontally some 600 yards southward. You can walk it today, sloshing along by candlelight or flashlight. Candlelight is better. The flame sputters and sometimes goes out. You hear voices, and reason says there is light somewhere at the end of the tunnel. But for a long moment, utter darkness and damp stone walls freeze the heart.

In 1867 the explorer Charles Warren discovered a vertical access, a zigzagging, sloping tunnel with steps; it leads from the City of David under the city wall to a shaft above Gihon's waters. For three seasons

Yigal Shiloh, helped by mining engineers and mountain climbers, had clawed at the soft fill that choked Warren's Shaft—slow and hazardous work. Now, for weeks Monteith and his co-workers have been hauling buckets of soil up and out, and they have broken through. At last we can follow the twisting, 160-foot path that once allowed besieged Jerusalemites to draw spring water. Israel hopes to make the passage a major attraction in an archaeological park.

For Keith Monteith, a Southern Baptist minister from North Carolina, toiling at the City of David has made the Bible narratives "really come alive." Back home at the seminary, the story of Adonijah's palace plot had puzzled him. Adonijah's plans, Bathsheba's appeal to David, Solomon's triumph at Gihon—all had to have occurred very swiftly. Was it possible? Here at the dig, seeing the proximity of the sites, he realized that the quick interplay of plot and counterplot could well have happened "in that dramatic way."

*T*o the City of David, states the Bible, Solomon added the Temple, a palace for himself, and another for the Egyptian wife he had taken. The Temple and its successor were destroyed; the existing Western Wall, part of King Herod's grandiose expansion of the Temple Mount in Roman days, was built nearly a thousand years after Solomon.

What of the palaces? The late Dame Kathleen Kenyon, a leading biblical archaeologist who dug at the City of David in the 1960s, believed that the royal complex had stood on the crest of the hill between the city and the Temple. But conquest and quarrying had taken their toll. "No actual remains of Solomonic Jerusalem have survived," she wrote.

Now it seems that some part of Solomonic Jerusalem *has* survived. It has been there, in plain view, for some time—a massive stonework sloping down from the crest of the City of David hill. Dr. Kenyon had identified it as a stepped glacis—a defensive incline—from the second century B.C. Now the new probe has exposed a lower part of the stone slope—and found it running *under* houses and pottery of the seventh and sixth centuries B.C. Behind and below the "glacis" lie pre-Israelite Canaanite remains from the 14th and 13th centuries. Sandwiched that way, the stone slope very likely dates from the golden years of the monarchy. If so, then Solomon, the biblical patron of the city's splendor, would probably have been the builder of this structure that rises more than five stories high. It may have been part of the internal defenses of the citadel, or the base of a monumental building.

Yigal Shiloh stressed its nearness to the Temple Mount, in that area seen as the probable site of Solomon's royal quarter. Whatever its purpose, the great stone slope holds a unique place in Israeli archaeology.

Until this discovery, said Shiloh, "no monumental construction that was preserved to such a height has been uncovered in Israel in any other biblical city."

The golden moment of David and Solomon is in itself unique. I heard that assessment during a delightful hour in which Dr. Abraham Malamat let go on the subject with his Roman-candle mind. Never before in history, said Malamat, a biblical historian at Hebrew University, and never since has there existed a Jerusalem-based empire of such size. The Israelite age, he said, arrived during a breakdown in power among the empires in Egypt and Mesopotamia. This loosened their grasp on the "buffer" lands between the Nile and the Euphrates. With what Malamat calls a "grand strategy" of military and organizing skills, David overcame all rivals among the small states; and when no superpower interfered, the kingdom evolved by Solomon's reign into the most important Near Eastern empire of its time.

During this greatest period in Israel's existence, however, there is no mention of it in external sources. Malamat suggests a reason. When Israel was strong, its neighbors were weak. The archives of Mesopotamia and Egypt are notably reticent when the home team loses. Furthermore, Israel's potential rivals must have regarded it with great suspicion. "The Phoenicians with their skills and craftsmanship," said Malamat, "what would they think of this backward land, *nouveau riche*, suddenly rising to power? I think Hiram of Tyre must have belittled David and Solomon, then tried very hard to get on with them."

Solomon's peerless wealth and wisdom? Perhaps "exaggerated, hyperbolic," said the professor, though the overall picture seems valid. He rejects the stereotype of a passive or decadent Solomon, a long drop from the heroic David: "They were much closer in kind. In my opinion it was a shift in emphasis. With David the emphasis was on war, with Solomon on

Contemporary picture and words 3,000 years old tell of harvest at Gezer. American volunteers at Kibbutz Gezer gather the melons of midsummer. Found in the ruins of the ancient city nearby, the Gezer "calendar" —one of the oldest known Hebrew epigraphs, probably a ditty for children and scribed in limestone around the time of Solomon—tolls the agricultural year: "His two months are planting; . . . His month is harvest and feasting; . . . His month is summer fruit."

RIGHT: MEHMET BIBER
CALENDAR ABOUT 4½ INCHES LONG

commerce. Solomon was not the unhappy successor who frittered away his legacy."

The united kingdom died with Solomon around 925 B.C. Jeroboam established the breakaway northern kingdom of Israel, while Solomon's son Rehoboam ruled Judah from Jerusalem. Solomon's costly splendors and levies of forced labor had stirred discontent. The First Book of Kings also cites divine wrath at his lust for foreign women: "Solomon clave unto these in love. And he had seven hundred wives, princesses, and three hundred concubines: and his wives turned away his heart." The Bible cites not the numbers as the cause of offense but the women's pagan worship. Solomon allowed it, even succumbed to it.

In the biblical indictment Dr. Malamat reads a testament to Solomon's power. "That's one of the symbols of real power," he said to me, "to enter into marriages of royal blood. In this I don't see anything shocking. The rule that you should marry a Jewish wife is a late rule and doesn't go for kings. These were marriages on the highest level of empire building."

As Israel's power radiated, so did its culture. One brilliant facet, Malamat suggested, was in Hebrew literature. Many scholars believe that scribes of the united monarchy—likely royal scribes in Solomon's bureaucracy—first set down the narratives that would grow into the books of the Old Testament.

Just off Jaffa Road in west Jerusalem I watched a bearded scribe, or *sofer*, carefully ink his goose quill and bend to his parchment. His shoulders were tensed, his forehead damp; he was copying the Pentateuch, the five books of Moses, for a new Torah scroll. In Jewish law it is a sacred, exacting task. The scribe began the day with a visit to the *mikvah*, the ritual baths. His quills come only from kosher birds, his parchment from the hides of kosher animals. An error in writing the name of the Deity cannot be corrected; the sheet must go to the *genizeh*, a special depository for old or damaged Torahs.

It takes the scribe ten minutes to write a line, some eighteen months to make a new Torah. Little wonder. The Torah will be read and re-read and revered in a synagogue. When kingdoms fell and temples lay in ruins, the Torah emerged, comfort and guide, accompanying the people of Israel wherever the centrifuge of history dispersed them.

Queen of Sheba's radiant visit has inspired artists of many periods and cultures. She and Solomon highlight a Persian rug captioned in Hebrew; its side panels depict symbols of Israel's tribes. One, the lion of Judah, also applies to Ethiopian kings; they traced descent from Solomon and the queen, a union portrayed in the goatskin scroll at upper right. A medieval manuscript, lower right, sees the queen as the Church, receiving wisdom from Christ, the "true Solomon."

UPPER: SIMON ROBERTON; LOWER: PHOTOGRAPH COURTESY THE BRITISH LIBRARY

"*Behold, thou art fair, my love; behold, thou art fair. . . . Thy lips are like a thread of scarlet. . . . Thy neck is as a tower of ivory.*" The words, from the Song of Solomon; the bride, Esther Matuf, from a community rooted in the Yemenite village of Habban, now living near Tel Aviv; the silver, from the craft of the village smiths. Incense (below) hangs heavy in the nuptial air—another legacy from southern Arabian lands where frankincense and myrrh grow. Trade in these fragrances, scholars think, sent the Queen of Sheba to Solomon's court. Legends of the Habbani trace their origins to that visit.

*F*rom the layer cake of Megiddo—
twenty levels of occupation from early
fourth millennium to fourth century
B.C.—came a choice bit of icing: this
chambered city gate, hallmark of
Solomon's royal architect. The relic
still guards Megiddo, where a path

below at left leads into the mound, today a national park. Near its right edge visitors can descend the dark circle of the famed water tunnel, built by King Ahab and featured in James Michener's novel The Source. *From Ahab's time, too, date hollowed and pierced stones that suggest mangers and posts of horse stables.*

FOLLOWING PAGES: *Designed for defense, the grand gateway of an Israelite city takes on the everyday look of marketplace, town square, open-air municipal center. A caravan arrives with pottery from Cyprus. A politician pleads for support. A disputant, arm raised, brings a legal case "unto the elders of the city in the gate"—as the Bible instructs.*

"*Now therefore command thou
that they hew me cedar trees out of
Lebanon.*" *Solomon placed his order;
King Hiram of Tyre replied:* "*I will
convey them by sea in floats unto the
place that thou shalt appoint me.*"
*The First Book of Kings cites a
familiar shipping technique, depicted
in an Assyrian relief (above) of the
eighth century* B.C. *The Phoenician port
of Tyre supplied much of Solomon's
building material, and came to
dominate Mediterranean commerce.
Cedar, a basic export, then swathed
the Lebanese hills, but centuries
of logging left only a few relic groves
such as this one. Lebanon calls the
gnarled survivors* "*Cedars of the Lord.*"

ABOVE: ERICH LESSING/MAGNUM

Ritual and sacred writ endure in Jerusalem, where King Solomon dedicated a temple to his God thirty centuries ago. In a pious quarter of the city a scribe letters Hebrew words of the Five Books of Moses as he prepares a new Torah scroll in a manner prescribed

by Jewish sages. He must not trust to memory, but follows precisely the printed copy guide, using ritually clean parchment, quill, and ink. Opposite, a participant holds a Torah during morning worship at the Western Wall. As sacred law requires, he wears a prayer shawl with tassels on the corners "that ye may look upon . . . and remember all the commandments." He also wears phylacteries—small leather boxes containing scriptural passages strapped to his left arm and forehead—"for a sign unto thee upon thine hand, and for a memorial between thine eyes, that the Lord's law may be in thy mouth."

POMPEII:

By Thomas O'Neill
Photographed by David Hiser

During its lifetime of six or seven centuries, the ancient town of Pompeii in the Campanian region of southern Italy won almost no historical notice. We can read that in 310 B.C. a Roman fleet under the command of Publius Cornelius landed at Pompeii and dispatched its men to pillage the countryside. The historian Tacitus recorded that in A.D. 59 the Roman Senate closed the Amphitheater at Pompeii to gladiator bouts for ten years, after a riot between the local populace and citizens of a rival town. Pliny the Elder praised Pompeian wine even though it afflicted him with hangovers. Such products as flowers, cabbages, and onions found favor in several texts. Yet when all had been written, Pompeii remained little more than a busy provincial town at the mouth of the River Sarnus, 12 miles southeast of Naples.

Today, of course, Pompeii is one of the most famous places in the world. To achieve such renown, it first had to vanish. This it did suddenly and tragically in August of the year 79, when the volcano Vesuvius exploded. The vineyard-wrapped mountain, a little less than six miles northwest of Pompeii, had been all but dormant for more than 1,200 years, and its fires were assumed to be long extinguished. On August 24, with little warning, it blasted its pent-up fury skyward, sending over the adjacent plain great sun-blackening clouds of pumice and ash.

Nearly a fifth of Pompeii's inhabitants — about 2,000 in a population estimated at 10,000 to 12,000 — are thought to have perished. Some died inside the town, crushed by collapsing roofs or falling columns on August 24 or suffocated by relentless rushes of hot ash and gases the next day. Many others died on the roads nearby, or drowned in the heaving, wind-tortured sea. When the eruption finally ceased, Pompeii was buried under volcanic debris more than 15 feet deep. Herculaneum, eight miles away, was also destroyed.

As time passed, the spot Pompeii once claimed became agricultural land indistinguishable from its surroundings except for a modest farm town. Even the name Pompeii was forgotten. The area came to be known as La Civita, from the Latin *civitas* meaning "state" or "city," in token recognition that there was once a thriving urban center here.

For more than 15 centuries the ruins remained concealed. In the late 1500s, architect Domenico Fontana tunneled through La Civita to channel water from the river—by now called the Sarno—to a nearby town. He was amazed to unearth several ancient buildings with inscriptions and fragments of brightly painted frescoes. No one fully comprehended the significance of Fontana's discovery, however; and not until 1748 did exploration of the mysterious buried city begin in earnest. At last in 1763, with the finding of an inscription containing the words *rei publicae Pompeianorum*, the site was identified as Pompeii.

The discovery of the lost city captivated the world. Every year or two of digging uncovered another dazzling patrician house or columned public building; many contained jewels, statues, or other valuable artifacts abandoned in the frenzy of evacuation. The mantle of volcanic material had proved an excellent preservative. When the temple of the Egyptian goddess Isis was exhumed in 1765, laborers found fish and eggs on a dining table. In one of the neighborhood bakeries, 81 loaves of bread were waiting in the oven. Inch by inch, an entire city was coming to light. Here was intimate physical evidence of Roman society, of daily life that previously had been revealed only in the pages of ancient literature.

Pompeii soon became a requisite stop on the Grand Tour of Europe. Visitors included Great Britain's Queen Victoria and Bavaria's King Ludwig I, who modeled one of his villas after a house he saw in Pompeii. The American general William Tecumseh Sherman paid a visit at the end of the Civil War. And novelists and poets were drawn to Pompeii from across the world.

Now, more than two centuries after its reemergence, Pompeii continues to mesmerize its visitors. It is a ruin unique for its variety and extent—a city complete with public buildings, miles of streets, hundreds of houses. There are neighborhoods for the aristocrats, neighborhoods for the tradesmen. There are temples, theaters, baths, brothels, and bars.

The town is not a haunting, windswept mausoleum. Because its demise was so sudden, Pompeii retains an air of immediacy and vibrancy that caused one 19th-century traveler to write of its "secret power that captivates . . . the soul. . . . We range through the same streets, tread the very same pavement, behold the same walls, enter the same doors" as those who dwelt here. Graffiti on the walls still exhort passersby; utensils resting on hearths appear usable; houses look inviting with their cool recesses and quiet gardens. The town is at once a museum for the study of life during Roman times and a theater for the imagination.

During my month-long visit to Pompeii, I often climbed to the top of the tower at the northern end of

Tour group leaves Pompeii's Forum through a stately arch built during the early years of the Roman Empire. The extensive ruins of the excavated city, among Italy's prime attractions, draw thousands of visitors each year.

PRECEDING PAGES: *Sunset tinges the Forum's broken columns, empty pedestals, and shattered buildings, memorials to the once flourishing Roman town. All activity ended here in August of the year 79, when Mount Vesuvius buried Pompeii under tons of pumice and ash. In the distance the volcano—for the moment, at least—broods in silence.*

Villa
of the Mysteries

Via dei Sepolcri

Unexcavated

House of
Obellius Firmus

House of the Vettii

Via di Mercurio

House of
the Faun

House of Pol

Baths

Via Stabiana

Bakery of Modestus

Fullery of
Stephanus

House of the
Tragic Poet

Baths

Lupanar

Thermopoliur

Baths

Via dell' Abbondanza

Forum

Temple of Isis

Theat

ITALY

0 KILOMETERS 200
0 STATUTE MILES 100

•Rome

Naples• ╀ *Mt. Vesuvius*
         ▫ POMPEII

Sardinia

Tyrrhenian Sea

Sicily

*Pompeii today: Maze-like map reveals a network of
mostly straight streets and narrow blocks packed with
houses and business premises. A partially excavated
wall, originally built for defense, surrounds the town.
Once an agricultural hamlet, Pompeii had grown to
nearly 12,000 inhabitants by A.D. 79. Although a
quarter of its area remains unexcavated, archaeologists
have discovered here a wealth of information about
everyday life in Roman times.*

PLAN OF POMPEII BASED ON MAP BY DR. HANS ESCHEBACH

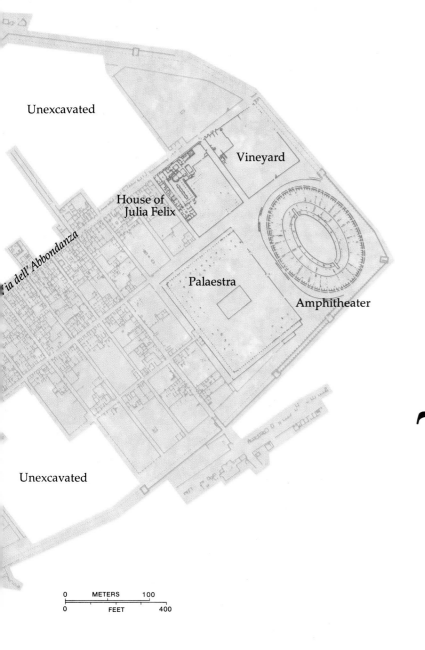

Unexcavated

Vineyard

House of
Julia Felix

Via dell' Abbondanza

Palaestra

Amphitheater

Unexcavated

```
0         METERS    100
0            FEET      400
```

of Naples region from the eighth to the end of the fifth century B.C. when an energetic Italic race called the Samnites, related to the original inhabitants, descended from the central mountains and overwhelmed Campania, taking control of its towns.

By 300 B.C. Rome was gradually but steadily enlarging its sphere of influence, and the Samnite town of Pompeii fell under its sway. Still, Pompeii maintained its autonomy, and as an ally of Rome, able to take advantage of new trade contacts, it evolved into a prosperous country town.

During the Social War of 91-87 B.C., Pompeii took the side of the Italic insurgents, but Roman troops defeated the uprising. In 80 B.C. Pompeii formally became a colony of Rome. By the time Vesuvius erupted in A.D. 79, Latin had replaced Oscan, the Samnite tongue, as the principal language, and the town had adopted the laws and absorbed much of the culture of Imperial Rome.

The Forum is the place to begin taking in the magic of ancient Pompeii. From the tower where I stand, the Via di Mercurio leads directly to the Forum, a large open space about the size of a football field. Off to the north, behind me, is the brooding bulk of Vesuvius; to the south are the sharp-spined Lattari Mountains, which drop into the Tyrrhenian Sea. In the Forum about a dozen large public buildings have survived, an unusually fine collection for a provincial town. In front of several of the buildings there remains a row of columns, some with entablatures and portions of an upper gallery still intact — the remnant of a grand two-story colonnade that extended part way around the public square. According to the late Amedeo Maiuri, eminent director of the Pompeii excavations from 1924 to 1961, the Pompeii Forum architecturally is "the most perfect and most grandiose" known to us from the Roman world. It takes only a few busloads of tourists spilling into the Forum to help my imagination create the stir of activity that once reigned here, the central gathering place for the town's residents.

The focal point of the Pompeii Forum was the Temple of Jupiter, at its northern end. It was an imposing building, its pediment supported by Corinthian columns 28 feet high. The temple's ruined state is due less to the volcanic eruption than to an earthquake that struck in A.D. 62, toppling Jupiter's sanctuary and leaving scarcely any building in town undamaged. Almost the entire Forum was undergoing reconstruction when Vesuvius blew up 17 years later.

Several municipal buildings stood at the Forum's southern end. In the southwest corner rose the Basilica, Pompeii's most impressive public structure. Its lofty interior was divided by columns into a broad hall and two side aisles—a stately design that would

the Via di Mercurio and looked out over the ruins. The town was compactly laid out, encompassing within its walls 155 acres. Three-fourths of the area has been excavated thus far. A patchwork of vegetable gardens covers the still buried northern section. Looking toward the heart of the city, however, I could gaze down on a honeycomb of building walls, the bare stone tinted brown under the hazy southern Italian sky. Here and there a faded orange tile roof identified a house that had undergone restoration. But what most attracted my eye were the columns. In every neighborhood they rise in solemn rows from the weeds, marking the former courts and gardens where they once supported roofs. In their number and impressive height, the columns stand as dignified reminders of Pompeii's proud and vigorous life.

Pompeii is thought to have been settled before the sixth century B.C. by a simple agricultural people. Greek and Etruscan ascendancy alternated in the Bay

profoundly influence the evolution of large Christian churches. This building served as a courtroom, a market, and a banking and trade center.

Other principal buildings in the Forum were the *macellum*—a partially covered food market—and the equally large Building of Eumachia, thought to be the guild hall and market for the area's woolen industry and built by its patron, Eumachia, a successful entrepreneur and one of the most prominent women in Pompeii's history.

Despite the ruined condition of the buildings, the design and purpose of the Forum are still vitally conveyed. A series of paintings from the House of Julia Felix, another businesswoman, depicts the multitude of activities that took place there. A visit to the Forum by Edward Bulwer-Lytton inspired many of the vivid scenes in his romantic novel *The Last Days of Pompeii*, which at the time—1834—rivaled the books of the preeminent Sir Walter Scott in popularity.

From the Forum, I could quickly step more intimately into Pompeian life by exploring the neighborhoods. North of the town square lies one of the more elegant sections, where many of the wealthy merchants and town patricians lived. It is called Region VI, a classification given by Giuseppe Fiorelli, director of excavations from 1860 to 1875, who imposed order on the study of Pompeii in part by indexing the town—numbering each region, block, and entryway.

The first time I walked the narrow, uneven streets of Region VI, I was struck by the severity of the house facades, which were flush with the sidewalk and unbroken by any feature other than tall, austere doors and a few small windows. Clearly the houses were intended as sanctuaries from the social commotion on the streets. Inside, the typical house opened into a lofty court called an atrium. The ceiling of the atrium rose twenty to thirty feet high, and in its middle was a rectangular opening called a compluvium, which allowed the entrance of light and air as well as rainwater. The latter was collected in a tank—the impluvium—and stored in an underground cistern for household use. Around the sides of the atrium were small rooms used for dining or sleeping. In one corner I sometimes found a lararium, a shrine to the household gods,

where the family sacrificed a tòken portion of a meal each day in hope of protection and good fortune.

The few furnishings included wooden cupboards and couches, oil lamps, and charcoal braziers for heat. An ornate metal strongbox called an *arca*, containing the household's valuables, often stood in the atrium.

The earliest form of the Pompeian house included simply the atrium, a smaller second room, or tablinum, and a vegetable garden in the back. By the second century B.C., the Samnites, influenced by Hellenistic styles, extended the house by converting the garden area into a peristyle, an open-air court with a colonnaded portico opening onto rooms. While the Greeks paved the floor of the peristyle, the Italics retained the garden's soil surface, thus creating the most important innovation of what became known as the Roman house: a wonderful open space full of light and plants, and ringed by elegant pillars. Some owners planted formal gardens with specially arranged flower beds and splashing fountains. Others combined beauty with practicality by growing fruit trees and vegetables alongside the flowers.

Pompeians spent much of their time outdoors, just as the people of southern Italy do today, and the peristyle became the most popular space in the house. Here the women could spin wool, the children could play with their pets, or a guest might read in the shade of a fig tree. It must have been a delightful scene when a family, reclining at dinner on marble couches, could look out over the garden where flowers scented the air, musicians piped on their instruments, and a fountain played its gay accompaniment.

Among the noble dwellings in Region VI is the House of the Faun. Considered the most beautiful existing example of ancient living quarters, the house—named after its statuette of a dancing faun—took up an entire block and contained two atriums and two peristyles, in addition to extensive mosaic work that is now in the National Archaeological Museum at Naples. Other notable residences include the House of the Tragic Poet, a compact, well-decorated home typical of those of the upper middle class; the House of the Silver Wedding, with four magnificent columns holding up the atrium ceiling; and the House of the Golden Cupids, a Roman-period structure with the west end of the peristyle raised like a theater stage.

The wealthy Pompeians greatly enjoyed being surrounded by color. The style of interior decoration was not to hang easel paintings, but instead to paint the entire wall. I would walk into a house, turn into one of the small bedrooms off the atrium, and see before me a wall surface flooded with vivid planes of primary colors framing *(Continued on page 115)*

Plaster images of a mother and child lie where they fell, overcome, on the road to safety (opposite). Behind them, workmen cautiously expose similar casts of other victims of Vesuvius's violent eruption. On August 24, A.D. 79, a great black cloud descended on Pompeii, covering the area with more than 15 feet of volcanic debris. Wisely, most people fled. The next day, hot gases and ash surging along the ground at speeds as high as 70 mph suffocated and buried those who remained. Eventually their bodies decayed, leaving detailed cavities in the compacted ash. In the mid-1800s, Giuseppe Fiorelli developed the technique of filling the cavities with plaster to re-create the forms of the victims in their last tragic moments. Examples of the process comprise an exhibit in the House of the Cryptoporticus, or underground room (below). These two victims took shelter with other inhabitants in the cellar. On August 25, believing the danger past, they made their way out to the garden only to die under the killing ash.

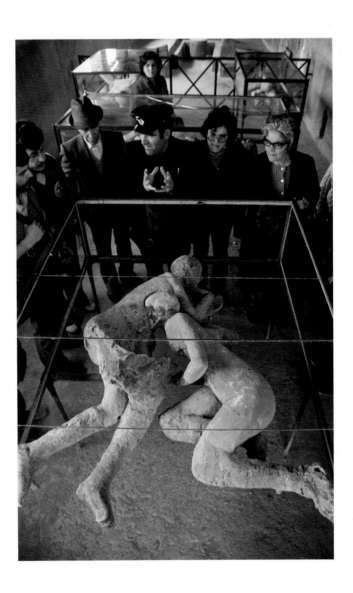

*H*ouse of M. Obellius Firmus, a large home of typical Pompeian design, sits in the lee of higher, unexcavated fields and gardens. Cubical rooms for dining, sleeping, bathing, and cooking surround a four-columned atrium. A colonnaded peristyle and a vegetable garden complete the lavish home. About two miles from Pompeii, excavators cut through more than 15 feet of volcanic debris (above) to expose a villa at ancient Oplontis. Farmers and gardeners, like the woman tying tomato vines to stakes, cultivate the fertile soil of the area's volcanic cover.

*E*mergency bracing supports shop fronts along Pompeii's Via dell'Abbondanza after severe earthquake shocks in November 1980. Temporarily barred to tourists, the city later reopened in some sections. At work several months before the tremors struck, laborers in the grand atrium of the House of Epidius Rufus (below) position a capital on its fluted column. Volcanoes and earthquakes have plagued this region since prehistoric times. Pompeii itself rests on an ancient lava flow. In A.D. 62 a violent quake toppled buildings and statues, severed the aqueduct, and damaged many pieces of art. The ruined state of the buildings today results as much from that earthquake as from the eruption of Vesuvius 17 years later.

animated figures—a startling sight in a ruined town. Most of the wall decorations have disappeared, torn out by earlier excavators and carted off to museums, principally at Naples. Others have faded away under the assault of sun, rain, and weeds. But enough remain to let us appreciate this remarkable art in its rightful setting.

Motifs of the murals are varied. They include brightly colored imitations of marble veneer and depictions of architectural features such as pilasters and porticos. Subjects from mythology and delightful landscape scenes also are numerous. The latter were an innovation of Roman art and, like the architectural paintings, were intended to create in a room an illusion of spaciousness.

Quality was uneven; most of the painters were workaday artisans whose job was to create a pleasing effect on their patrons' walls. But in general their results showed considerable charm, and a few paintings achieved unqualified excellence—including the frieze "Dionysian Mysteries," a large mural that was uncovered in 1930 at the Villa of the Mysteries and has been called by some the finest example of classical wall art. The background color is the famous Pompeii red, a deep ruddy hue that still looks fresh 2,000 years after it was applied.

Judging by the homes of the prosperous citizens, it seems obvious that a good share of Pompeii's population vigorously pursued a luxurious life style. When the gentry weren't managing their estates or relaxing at home, they could often be found in congenial conversation at the Forum or being washed and perfumed at one of the public baths. An inscription found on one mosaic reads: "Death plucks my ear and says, 'Live! for I come.'"

If the pursuit of pleasure played a recurring chord in Pompeian life (Petronius' *Satyricon* was set in a fictional Campanian town not unlike Pompeii), then the fondness for enterprise supplied the basic rhythm. The words *Salve Lucrum*—"Hail Profit"—appear on the mosaic floor tile in the vestibule of one merchant's house. In this busy port town, shops were sprinkled through almost every block.

What is now identified as Region VII, east of the

Heart of a Pompeian home, this luxurious peristyle garden draws the household to its refreshing coolness. Two women sip wine from a local vineyard while curious children watch a slave prepare the afternoon meal on an improvised stove. Although the recent earthquake has damaged the kitchen, priority goes to repairing the peristyle; roofers, painters, and plasterers finish mending the effects of the quake. Here, from dawn to dusk, family members worked, played, worshiped, and dined with the scent of fragrant flowers and the music of moving water.

Forum, was the most densely populated part of town. It was also the nucleus of the original settlement, and its cramped, narrow streets—like those in the Spacca Quarter, the old district of Naples—contrast with the orderly grid patterns of the rest of Pompeii. The homes generally are not the spacious, atrium-peristyle mansions found in Region VI. These houses belonged to the common people, and consist of small, undecorated, irregular rooms inhabited today by furtive green lizards, broom grass, and Queen Anne's lace.

The commercial operations of Pompeii are fascinating primarily because this aspect has been documented so rarely in other excavated towns. But they also appeal because, in a setting dominated by singular, often extravagant temples and mansions, the sight of a tavern or a bakery brings with it a sense of familiarity and everyday reality in the midst of near-fanciful surroundings.

The most easily identified shops are the thermopoliums, with their L-shaped masonry counters for the serving of refreshments. Few street corners were without them; more than a hundred such bars have been counted in Pompeii. The counters held large earthenware jars containing food and wine. Pompeians were particularly fond of heated wine. Some of these shops also had kitchens that prepared hot stew; others boasted back rooms where customers could sit and talk and perhaps gamble while they drank.

As a port city, Pompeii received a steady stream of foreign visitors. Some twenty hotels have been found. The largest is located in Region VII. It could accommodate fifty guests, and had a garden for outdoor dining.

Another common sight is a bakery, recognizable by its oven and large, hourglass-shaped grinding mills. Bread replaced cereal porridge as a staple food in Italy by the second century B.C.; and 33 bakeries or related shops have been identified in Pompeii.

The chief exports were wine, olive oil, a pungent fish sauce known as *garum*, and woolen goods. Thirty-nine wool-processing plants, or fulleries, have been discovered in the town.

In his popular guidebook, director Maiuri speculated that Region VII had a negative reputation because of its "questionable inns" and gambling rooms. One householder scratched on his outside wall the Latin words *Otiosis locus hic non est: discede morator*—"This is no place for idlers: loiterer, be off!" Prostitution evidently was commonplace in Pompeii, not surprising in a town frequented by foreign merchants and sailors far from home. A well-preserved, two-story *lupanar*, or brothel, today is often jammed with tittering tourists who peer into the cell-like rooms, furnished only with small stone beds and decorated above the doorways with a series of lascivious paintings.

Skylit atrium welcomes visitors to the reconstructed House of the Vettii (right). Rain, falling through the opening into the impluvium, supplied the household with water before Pompeii installed a system of pipes leading from an aqueduct. Beyond the atrium beckoned the peristyle with its green plants, garden furniture, and decorative sculpture—

including a dazzling array of statues jetting water into marble basins. At another house, the triclinium at left looked out on a delightful view of the garden. Three benches made comfortable with cushions gave the Roman dining arrangement its name. Bronze pots and pans rest on a kitchen hearth, typically located at a distance from the triclinium to keep diners as cool as possible. Cave canem—"Beware of the dog"—reads an entryway floor mosaic that leaves the present custodian's pet unimpressed.

121

The emphasis of research nowadays, the surprisingly young—29—de Caro pointed out, is to "publish Pompeii"; in other words, to document the buildings in detail, an essential effort because early excavation reports were so hopelessly inadequate.

"The task is to publish the excavations systematically," he said. "Publishing is a way of restoring. To make good restorations depends on knowing as exactly as possible what was in the house and all the precise dimensions of the building."

Although the Italian government has suspended most excavation within the city walls, nevertheless some important digging has been undertaken in recent years, largely by an American who has chosen to uncover not buildings but gardens. Dr. Wilhelmina Jashemski, professor emeritus of ancient history at the University of Maryland, has traveled to Pompeii for more than twenty summers to study the plots which she believes illuminate much about life there in the first century. Thus far, with the aid of her husband, Stanley, a physicist and photographer, Dr. Jashemski has identified and documented some 450 gardens. She has studied them in the peristyles of mansions, in the corners of three-room houses, in restaurants, inns, temples, and tombs. Often she and her work crew have had to slash through treelike weeds to be able simply to locate the plot. Her method of study involves making Fiorelli-style casts of ancient roots, and obtaining analyses of pollen samples and of carbonized wood, seeds, and fruit in order to identify the plants that grew in a particular garden.

In her distinguished work *The Gardens of Pompeii*, published in 1979, Dr. Jashemski presented her theory that the garden, modest as it may seem, stood in "intimate relation . . . to almost every aspect of ancient Roman life — to architecture, painting, aesthetic expression, horticulture, economics, city-planning, and religion." For the individual family, she believes, the garden came to be the soul of the house.

Her most exciting find took place in the mid-1960s, a result of a determined hunch. North of the Amphitheater is a large open plot that takes up an entire city block and was identified as a cattle market. Curious as to whether this extensive area had once been planted, especially since a two-room wine-making complex had been discovered during excavations in the 1950s, Dr. Jashemski undertook subsoil examinations. Her first trench, dug four feet deep through volcanic debris to reach the ground level of A.D. 79, quickly produced a tree-root cavity. Heartened, she extended the digging. But after days of grueling work, she came up with little else, and was advised to give up because the scant results could not justify the expense

of the excavations. Yet she persisted; and after several more days of frustration, she exposed eight evenly spaced cavities, followed by another row, and another, until she reached one of the street walls. Dr. Jashemski had come upon a large vineyard, the first ever found from antiquity.

When the digging was completed in 1970 (the lot has since been reclaimed by weeds), 2,014 vine-root cavities had been revealed. In succeeding years, she examined other puzzling open areas in the southeast section of town—Region I—where, between 1951 and 1961, the last extensive excavations in Pompeii had taken place. There she found a large market garden and a sizable orchard.

As a result of Dr. Jashemski's discoveries, the extent of Pompeii's city planning came into focus for the first time. Fully a third of the excavated city had been left to open space, the professor calculated, and it became apparent that a portion of the southeastern quarter had been reserved for gardens that supplied the town with some of its produce.

"Ancient Pompeii," Dr. Jashemski wrote, "with its many open areas of green—gardens, parks, vineyards, orchards, and vegetable plots—must have been very beautiful indeed, and very different from the crowded, overbuilt city sometimes described by modern scholars."

From the Amphitheater it is but a short distance to the 17-block-long Via dell'Abbondanza, or Street of Abundance, a fitting name for the excavators to have given the great commercial thoroughfare of Pompeii. Disinterred over the years from 1911 to 1941, the Via dell'Abbondanza represents a synthesis of modern excavating techniques learned since the time of Fiorelli.

What has surfaced is an avenue that seems to echo with its past activity. I see and touch the reconstructions of sliding wooden doors that closed the shops at the end of the day; I inspect the food counters where drinking vessels still rest on the polychrome marble surfaces, and the back rooms where the large, two-handled wine jugs, or amphorae, are stacked. Restored overhangs shade the sidewalk. Balconies, galleries, and second stories overlook the street. Public fountains stand at major intersections, and above the pavement rise the triads of large stepping stones once used by pedestrians to cross flooded streets. Paintings adorn the fronts of shops, their subjects ranging from divinities to craftsmen.

The most marvelous aspect of the street, though,

Bronze statuette of a dancing faun—a mythical figure with the body of a man and the ears, horns, and tail of a goat— once graced a fountain in Pompeii's grandest home, now known as the House of the Faun. Muscles taut, the semiwild creature prances exuberantly to music that only he can hear.

is the 2,000-year-old graffiti. Words and phrases appear on shops and houses in large stylized letters, exhorting the citizens (for instance) to vote for Lucius Popidius Secundus and, on the same wall, reminding them to see the gladiators of Gnaeus Alleius Nigidius Maius fight on June 13. Electoral inscriptions alone number more than 3,000 in Pompeii. Even more common, though difficult to read, are the casual comments inscribed on walls by the idle or the mischievous armed with a sharp-pointed stylus. Like the comparable scratchings of today, these hairline writings record all manner of passing thoughts, from amorous boasting to poetical musing. It is the graffiti, finally, that proclaim most eloquently the unquenchable life of the Via dell'Abbondanza and even of Pompeii as a whole, and force me to acknowledge the continuity of human qualities that make the most foreign of times and people become vividly recognizable.

One last time I walk the length of the Street of Abundance and end again at the Forum. As often before, I feel tired yet exhilarated: I have partaken of the serenity of a Roman ghost town where the weathered stones absorb time like heat, but I also sense an uncanny energy, as if I have walked through a crowded bazaar. The drama and the activity of the town come easily to my mind. The buildings and the streets, with their stories to tell, have practically taken on the roles of characters.

Despite the timeless tableaux, the evidence is everywhere, too, that the ages move inexorably onward. I look off toward the rim of Vesuvius and remember that it has erupted seventy times—most recently in 1944—since it buried Pompeii. Many houses still show damage from an Allied bombing raid in 1943, when warplanes tried to knock out nearby military targets. Inside many of the houses, summer workers take their scythes to the insidious weeds or start spading to replant the old gardens. In the mansion known as the House of C. Julius Polybius, on the Via dell'Abbondanza, workmen reattach to a wall a piece of a fallen painting showing a winged figure in flight. Solemn-looking men and women pose for wedding pictures in front of noble pillars, and a first-communion class runs through the Forum in Sunday dress.

When I finally depart the storied town, I leave behind a retreat suspended between timeless antiquity and the insistent presence of the modern world. The noise of the street traffic of the new Pompeii quickly snaps my spell, and the sensation of observing the distant past recedes as swiftly as do the buildings behind the sun-tinted walls. What does not leave me, that day and for many beyond it, is a rare, sustaining optimism, one that comes from having witnessed that the objects and visions of man can persist through time and still retain their power to instruct and entrance— even in a town that barely made the history books.

Finely wrought gold and silver artifacts illustrate the skill of ancient craftsmen. An arm band and a ring take the form of a serpent, a symbol believed to ward off bad luck and commonly found throughout Roman households. The bracelet

of gold hemispheres once graced the wrist of a Pompeian lady. Flowerlike, pearl "petals" radiate from the green-quartz centers of a pair of earrings. A twin-handled silver cup, found hidden away with a hoard of other tableware, boasts an elaborate motif of olive branches heavy with fruit. Mythological characters in miniature, highlighted with gold, enliven the handle of a silver bowl; relative simplicity distinguishes the small pitcher.

Fragile remnants of a bygone era still charm the beholder. On an amphora-shaped glass vase, grape vines and flowers frame cherubic winemakers crushing grapes to the music of a double flute. This intricate cameo style inspired the famous designs of the 18th-century English artisan Josiah Wedgwood. The technique of glass blowing, developed in the first century B.C., made much more affordable such articles of everyday use as the blue pitcher, pearl-white vase, and heavy chalice.

126

ALL BY VICTOR R. BOSWELL. JR.

FOLLOWING PAGES: *"You may take four giant steps." Visitor crosses a street on raised stones that left spaces for wheels of passing carts while allowing pedestrians to avoid running water.*

*W*arren-like confusion of walls divides private houses from bakeries, thermopoliums, brothels, inns, baths, workshops, a fish shop, fulleries, dye works, and a poultry shop near this once-busy intersection. The gymnastic ground of the Central Baths occupied the only open area. At the Forum Baths (above), a tourist stands beneath a skylight in the hot-bath room, or calidarium. A shrine to deities and to a guardian spirit fills the wall beyond the countertop receptacles of a thermopolium (right).

FOLLOWING PAGES: *Amused customers listen to the tall tale of the proprietor of a thermopolium selling warmed wine and light food. Next to a massive arch in the Via dell'Abbondanza stands the purple-cloaked statue of influential M. Holconius Rufus. Elsewhere in this artist's impression, men on their way to the baths carry strigils, implements to scrape off cleansing oil and dust; a slave draws water from a fountain; and a prosperous businessman heads homeward from the Forum.*

$\mathcal{L}$ava millstone—one of three—and a brick-faced oven furnish a large workroom in a typically equipped bakery. Most bakers milled their own grain, using donkeypower to rotate the hourglass-shaped stones. Flour accumulated on the circular shelf. The largest of 33 Pompeian baking establishments possessed five such mills. On Pompeii's last day, workers at the Bakery of Modestus placed 81 loaves of bread in the oven's immense baking compartment. There they remained for 18 centuries, protected and preserved (right) by the volcanic seal. Also found during excavation: eggs, nuts, and lentils. Today, bakers of the area continue to prepare the traditional round, eight-sectioned loaves and restaurateurs use ovens modeled along ancient lines.

*P*esce mangia pesce, *as the Italians say—it's a "fish eat fish" world, a philosophy suggested by this detailed and entertaining floor mosaic from a Pompeian home within sight and sound of the sea. At the center, an octopus's sinuous tentacles ensnare a hapless lobster. A variety of sea creatures swim about the struggle, seemingly oblivious to the drama. Pompeii, located in ancient times between the River Sarnus and the Tyrrhenian Sea, used fish and fish products both as staple foods and for trade. Below, an assortment for sale beside the Bay of Naples attests to seafood's undiminished popularity in southern Italy.*

Four speeding chariots vie for advantage in a race depicted in an unfinished mural. Although Pompeii had no permanent racetrack, it did have what scholars label the oldest amphitheater in the Roman world. Crowds of 20,000 gathered in the oval area to watch animal baiting and gladiatorial games. Spectators cheered their heroes, whose battles could end with the death of the loser unless the audience decreed clemency. The broad brim and visor of a bronze helmet (left), found in the gladiators' barracks, gave some protection to the combatant. Directly west of the Amphitheater, Pompeian youths trained and competed in the colonnaded athletic school called the Palaestra (below).

Two-story lupanar, Latin for brothel, dominates the sharply angled intersection of two narrow streets. Located in the oldest, most densely populated section of Pompeii, the lupanar entertained local residents as well as visiting merchants and foreign sailors. Inside, customers entered cubicles (below) furnished with cushion-covered masonry couches. Above, amatory couples dally in one of the many paintings found in the excavations. The seemingly uninhibited life-style of Pompeii convinced Victorian scholars that the city epitomized a decadent Roman society.

*P*ompeii's horseshoe-shaped Great Theater
and smaller Odeum gleam in early morning
sunlight. A movable awning shaded ancient
audiences in the Great Theater during
plays and public meetings. In the Odeum,
a permanent roof aided acoustics during
concerts. Originally modeled on Greek styles,
both structures existed in Pompeii before
Rome had its first permanent theater. Below,
a near-capacity crowd in the Great Theater
watches Aristophanes' Thesmophoriazusae
(or Festival of the Women). With two theaters,
an amphitheater, a variety of commercial
activities, and a remarkable number of
luxurious homes, the Pompeii of A.D. 79
reflected a comfortable and sophisticated
standard of living.

143

By Cynthia Russ Ramsay
Photographed by Michael S. Yamashita

THE MYSTERIOUS

KINGDOM OF KUSH

In the cruel African desert, under a hard blue sky, the ruins of the temple complex stood ravaged and forlorn in the wind-rippled sands. Broken columns, sections of sandstone walls, and crumbling sculptures were all that remained of the Great Enclosure—a huge maze of corridors, courtyards, and buildings unlike anything else anywhere in the world.

No one knows why the strange structure was built; its origin and purpose are long forgotten, lost in the vast stillness of the desolate land. Enigmatic inscriptions may refer to the Great Enclosure, but no one understands them. Though scholars can transliterate the characters into the Roman alphabet, fifty years of effort have failed to interpret the words, and the language remains an intractable mystery.

Nevertheless, archaeologists have sought to make sense of the elaborate complex, mustering such various explanations as a military academy, a school for training elephants, a ceremonial center for sacred festivals, and a summer palace for royalty.

I sensed the former splendor of the place as I walked past walls once sparkling with paint and pale plaster and paused before richly carved pillars now weathered and broken. I prowled in and out of countless passageways and gaping, roofless chambers with floors covered with sand. But the monuments evoked no specific images, for where I wandered might have been an elephant stable or a court where Roman ambassadors bowed before plump, imperious queens; it might have been the site of some magnificent festival or the scene of an unknown, still unfathomed event.

Nothing but the persistent buzz of flies disturbed the great brooding silence that hung over the ruins—a silence made more overwhelming by the knowledge that so much must have happened here.

With its alien, uncomprehended grandeur, the Great Enclosure at Musawwarat es-Sufra is the essence of mystery, and as such it symbolizes Meroë—the intriguing civilization that flourished along the River Nile in what the ancient Egyptians called the land of Kush, and the classical world knew as Aethiopia. In our day it lies within the northern third

Its unique and puzzling design leaves unexplained the purpose of the Great Enclosure at Musawwarat es-Sufra in the northern Sudan—an elaborate complex of temples, plazas, corridors, and ramps unparalleled elsewhere in the world. Archaeologists place construction of its colonnaded central temple in the first century A.D.

PAGES 144-145: *Ruins of Musawwarat es-Sufra silently testify to the intermingling of ancient cultures. Although geographically remote from the classical centers of civilization, the site has yielded inscriptions in Greek and Latin as well as Egyptian and the native Meroitic.*

of the Democratic Republic of the Sudan and the southernmost part of the Arab Republic of Egypt.

Archaeologists have spent lifetimes trying to solve the puzzles of Kush, a kingdom whose beginnings go back at least to the eighth century B.C. To some extent they have succeeded, rescuing from oblivion a civilization so mighty it briefly conquered ancient Egypt, battled the legions of Imperial Rome, and endured for a thousand years.

To learn what scholars have discovered, to view the monuments they have unearthed, I journeyed to abandoned, sand-choked cities along the Nile, to temples and palaces on the arid steppes of the region called the Butana, and to pyramid tombs where god-kings were buried with dazzling treasure.

The trail, sometimes just twin tire tracks in the sand, began in Khartoum, capital of the Sudan — largest country in Africa and more than one-fourth the size of the United States. On a warm January day, I became acquainted with that city of mosques, imposing British colonial mansions, and flat-roofed adobe houses. I roamed the outdoor bazaars with their narrow, twisting streets and followed the boulevard along the riverbank, shaded by great banyan trees. Later I lingered at the sprawling camel market in nearby Omdurman where seminomadic herdsmen sell their animals, prized by gourmets of the Persian Gulf. Because it was Friday, the Muslim Sabbath, the dervishes danced in the afternoon, swaying and gyrating to the incessant beat of drums and the soundless rhythms of their religious fervor.

Part African, part Arab and Middle Eastern, vaguely Mediterranean, Khartoum reflects the same marvelously eclectic yet independent spirit that characterized the Meroitic civilization.

"The Meroites borrowed religious beliefs, art, architecture, and hieroglyphics from the Egyptians but ultimately developed their own writing system, added their own gods to the pantheon, and interpreted Egyptian art motifs and models in their creative way," said Negm el Din Mohammed Sherif, Commissioner for Archaeology in the Sudan and my affable host at the National Museum. "They were also influenced by their contacts with the classical world of Greece and Rome."

We strolled across the handsomely landscaped garden. Near the doorway to the museum, a pair of statues towered above us. "Consider these two male figures, which were designed to stand at the entrance to a temple," said Negm el Din. "At first glance they seem Egyptian; but the proportions are stockier, the lips fuller, the faces flatter, and the costume and jewelry different and more elaborate. They are definitely Meroitic."

Once inside the museum, I discovered that the Meroites were no less versatile in giving Roman-inspired art their own strong southern accent. A

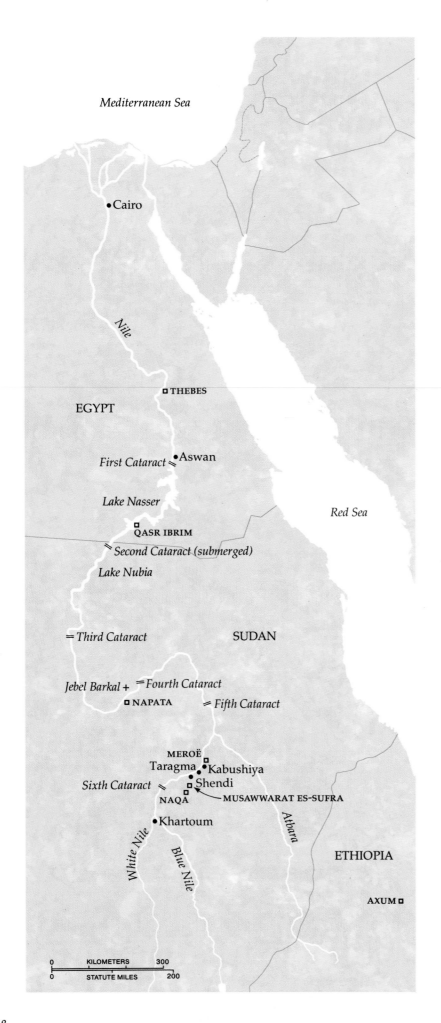

sandstone statue of a nude woman was obviously influenced by the Venus figures of Greece and Rome, but the wide hips, full thighs, straight shoulders, long neck, and hair in small, tight curls manifested another ideal of beauty and made clear that the artist was not slavishly copying the classical prototype.

A sandstone head with deep-set eyes, striking in its bold simplicity, attracted my attention. Abstract and highly stylized, the sculpture expressed still another aspect of Meroitic art—utterly African and tremendously appealing.

Ornaments of gold, silver, and copper crowded the glass cases—rings, pendants, earrings, armlets with two hinged segments; bead collars of glass, carnelian, and other semiprecious stones. The jewelry came from royal tombs that had been plundered long ago, and comprised objects the thieves had overlooked. For this reason the collection could give only an inkling of the enormous treasure that must have accompanied kings and queens to their graves.

We stopped before a display of Meroitic wheel-turned pottery, ranked by connoisseurs among the finest in the ancient world. Antelopes, lions, winged serpents, giraffes browsing on trees, pastoral scenes, and human caricatures—all gaily painted in a bold, vigorous style—decorated eggshell-thin bowls, bottles, goblets, and jars in shapes of amazing variety.

A cruder handmade ware served for beer pots and wine jars, and their great number provides ample evidence of how people liked to pass their time.

The art also speaks of countless battles. Scenes of bound captives and of Meroitic kings striking their enemies with their swords occur again and again in sculpture and in relief on temple walls. No one can say for certain who all the enemies were, but inscriptions written in Egyptian hieroglyphs refer to restless nomadic tribes filtering in from the eastern and western deserts and raiding along the kingdom's frontiers.

Warfare had been a way of life long before the Meroitic period. For centuries the people of the region resisted the armies of Egypt. As early as 2900 B.C., a pharaoh had mounted a military raid on the lands beyond the First Cataract of the Nile. Even though Egyptian wall paintings show dark-skinned southerners bearing such tribute as gold, animal skins, and ostrich eggs, local chieftains repeatedly challenged Egyptian authority. Nevertheless for almost 500 years,

Between Khartoum in the northern Sudan and Aswan in southern Egypt, the River Nile plunges through six cataracts—swift, steep rapids that preclude navigation. Among the granite hills and sand dunes that border the river's winding path lie the remains of the Meroitic civilization, named for the second capital of the Kingdom of Kush. The little-known monarchy endured from before 700 B.C. to about A.D. 350.

from about 1550 B.C., Kush was actually an occupied country, colonized by Egyptian civil servants, scribes, and priests. Yet all the while the pharaohs' soldiers were local warriors who hired out as mercenaries.

A policy of Egyptianization—educating the nobility in Egypt, and building temples to promulgate the cult of Amun, the state god—succeeded in winning the allegiance of Kushite leaders where the force of arms had failed. The profound Egyptian influence prevailed long after the empire had declined, and after the princes of Kush had won their independence. The capital of the new kingdom was at Napata, just below the Fourth Cataract of the Nile.

Napata had long been a center of Amun worship, and it was in the name of Amun and to restore Egypt's former glory that the first great Kushite king, Kashta, seized the famed Egyptian capital of Thebes. His son Piye (Piankhy) continued the crusade, mobilizing an army of archers, slingers, and swordsmen and a fleet of riverboats and barges. In 731 B.C. he marched out of Napata to complete the conquest of Egypt and to deliver the empire from the throes of civil war.

Piye founded the XXV Dynasty and took his place among a long line of Egyptian pharaohs. But the Kushites controlled Egypt for only 70 years, retreating to their homeland after Assyrian troops swept out of western Asia and struck deep into Egypt.

Thereafter in Napata a succession of monarchs perpetuated Egyptian traditions: commissioning art and literature, building pyramids, and raising temples to Amun, who was claimed as the divine ancestor of the Kushite god-kings. Not until the center of power shifted south to the city of Meroë in the sixth century B.C. did a new civilization with its own character and genius begin to take form.

I set out for Meroë, 120 miles north of Khartoum, with Saleh Omar es-Sadiq, tall, swarthy Inspector of Antiquities, and Ardemis Sahle, an Ethiopian refugee who was the owner and driver of our hired Land Rover. Our supplies included tea, a dark chewy bread, canned pineapple, cheese, mosquito repellent, and jerry cans of gasoline, for we could not count on buying petrol anywhere on our journey.

Minutes after we left Khartoum's heavy traffic behind, the asphalt pavement gave way to desert, and we jounced along trailing a wake of yellow dust. From time to time we lurched into places where the sand was soft and loose, but Ardemis always managed to coax his vehicle through. Although I caught fleeting glimpses of date palms marking the narrow fringe of fields nourished by the Nile, our route was across a woefully thirsty land, featureless but for clumps of yellow desert grasses, a scattering of small acacia trees, and occasional low, barren hills.

Rich variety and remarkable quality of craftsmanship distinguish the pottery uncovered in the region of Kush. An abundance of fine earthenware in even the humblest villages indicates that a general prosperity prevailed throughout the kingdom. Of the small pots below, the wheel-turned barbotine beaker at right, probably brought from Egypt, demonstrates provincial Roman style. The rare vessel at top, also wheel-turned, illustrates luxury ware of impressed design. The hand-built utilitarian pot at bottom shows the more traditional African style. All the wares pictured here date from the first to third centuries A.D.

VICTOR R. BOSWELL, JR.
POTS SHOWN APPROXIMATELY ½ ACTUAL SIZE

Golden ornaments overlooked by tomb plunderers suggest the considerable wealth of the Kingdom of Kush. Bits of fused glass inlaid in gold form the mosaic-like configurations of much Meroitic finery. The hinged armlets bearing winged goddesses came from the grave of powerful Queen Amanishakheto. Scarabs— beetle-shaped amulets— make up the gold chain at far left. The hinged shield of the ring at bottom left covered several fingers and knuckles. Rings of this type remain popular in the Sudan. At near left, a uraeus rising in front of the miniature canine figure represents the sacred serpent, symbol of royalty.

VICTOR R. BOSWELL, JR.

JEWELRY SHOWN APPROXIMATELY 1½ TIMES ACTUAL SIZE; FIGURINE ENLARGED 5 TIMES

As we lumbered along, I asked Saleh why the ancient capital had been transferred from Napata to Meroë. In reply he summarized the various theories of scholars, confirming once again that the story of Meroë is rife with uncertainties.

"Some believe the kings were trying to escape the power of the Amun priesthood entrenched in Napata.

"Some think the Napatans were drawn to the region by the climate, which was wetter than that of the virtually rainless north, and wetter than it is here today. The herdsmen would have found better pasture for their cattle, and farmers could raise larger crops of sorghum and other grains in the wadis [the usually dry watercourses] after the summer rains.

"There are those who argue the kings always came from Meroë, and resided there. Napata, they say, was never more than a religious center, where the king went for his coronation and burial.

"Others attribute Meroë's rise to trade. The site straddled the desert caravan routes going north, east, and southeast. And upriver from Meroë, the White Nile was navigable to the interior of Africa."

Centuries later, caravans again converged on virtually the same spot—just twenty miles south of Meroë in the age-old market town of Shendi. Here we spent the night at the Antiquities Department rest house.

The scene that surrounded me in Shendi's market — the men in long, loose *jellabias* and turbans or skullcaps, the women in veils that draped casually over the head without concealing the face, the open stalls with baskets of grain, the sides of beef hanging from hooks, the clangor of blacksmiths at their anvils —might have belonged to another century but for the few cars and trucks, the rubber tires on the horse-drawn carts, and the radios blaring Arab music.

The sun had burned away the cool of early morning by the time we headed north from Shendi into a desert that stretched off to the heat-dimmed horizon. Before long I discerned the cluster of small, steep pyramids of Meroë's North Cemetery. About a quarter mile away stood a smaller group marking the few royal burials in the South Cemetery.

In no way as imposing as the massive tombs of Egypt, many of the pyramids of Meroë nevertheless have a dainty elegance all their own. None is still complete. Most were 50 to 100 feet high, and comprised a masonry casing filled with rubble. In Meroë's final centuries, brickwork substituted for the stone mantle and the height was reduced to a mere 13 to 20 feet.

More than sixty royal pyramids stand above underground burial chambers at Meroë. The first ruler to be entombed here instead of in one of the royal cemeteries around Napata was Arkamani-qo, who died about 260 B.C. The change in burial site was

Among their technological achievements, the Meroites mastered basic iron-working (opposite). In the shade of an acacia tree, a blacksmith of the first century A.D. straightens a spearhead while a seated customer waits and a satisfied soldier inspects a finished arrow. The smith's apprentice works a bellows to keep the coals flaming. Facial scarring like the warrior's, originally a means of tribal identification, eventually became an important element of personal decoration (above) among the Ja'aliyin, descendants of the Meroites. Such scarification has become increasingly rare.

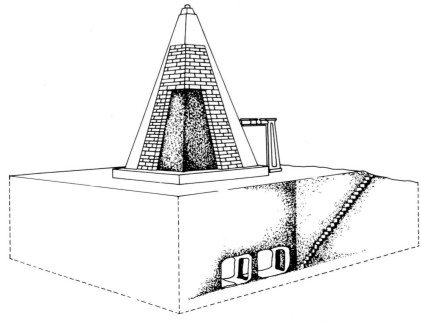

Although the Kushites, like the ancient Egyptians, erected pyramids to honor their royal dead, they placed the burial chamber beneath the superstructure (diagram at left) and filled the pyramid walls above ground with rubble. On the eastern side they built an offertory chapel. Meroë's cemeteries—two of them visible above—today form the largest collection of pyramids in the world.

probably tantamount to a coup d'etat against the priests of Amun. According to a Greek chronicle written two centuries later, these priests were so powerful that they commanded kings, could oust them, could even force them to commit suicide. The chronicle goes on to say that a monarch "who had a Greek education . . . put them to the sword, and . . . thereafter ordered affairs after his own will."

The pyramids of Napata and Meroë have provided a chronology for the Kingdom of Kush. The late American archaeologist George Reisner, who excavated there during the years from 1916 to 1923, assumed

that in each cemetery the first king raised his pyramid in the most commanding position and each successor took the next best site. By using this rationale and by studying the varying forms of burial and the changing styles of the pyramids, Reisner came up with a sequence of construction. He then took the names inscribed in the tombs and produced a chronology of kings that has been modified only slightly in the sixty years since it was so ingeniously devised.

Ingenuity, imagination, and painstaking labor involving an immense amount of detail continue to make inroads on the mysteries of Meroë — perhaps

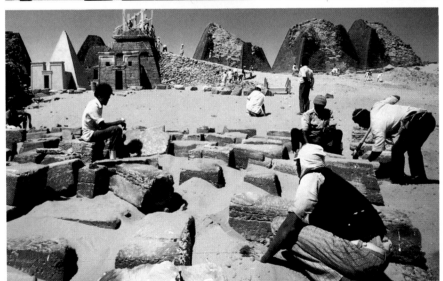

*R*econstruction of a pyramid and its offertory chapel progresses by such authentic early building methods as use of a continually enlarged rubble ramp and the shadoof, a lever system that hoists blocks weighing more than 400 pounds. Dr. Friedrich Hinkel (above, upper right), an architect and archaeologist in the Sudan for twenty years, supervises the project. Restoration of the partially eroded pyramid first required deconstruction, a painstaking process that included numbering the casing blocks according to level, then burying them in the sand for safekeeping.

*Desert sun sets beyond royal pyramids at Meroë.
Opposite, a highly stylized sandstone head, placed in
a tomb chapel to represent the deceased, now rests
in the National Museum at Khartoum. Archaeologists
characterize the head, discovered in lower Nubia and
assigned to the second to third century A.D., as one of
the finest and most unusual of Meroitic sculptures.*

nowhere more dramatically than in the work of Friedrich W. Hinkel of the Academy of Sciences of the German Democratic Republic. The Berlin architect is reconstructing several of the royal pyramids in the North Cemetery block by block and restoring the wall reliefs in the funeral chapels fragment by fragment.

"Until recently no one realized that the Meroitic pyramids were slightly truncated—flattened off at the top—or that they were plastered and painted with decorations," Hinkel said to me in his careful, clipped English. At the same time he continued directing a brigade of men who were setting a block precisely in place on a half-restored pyramid. They were hoisting the stone with an ancient lifting device called, in Arabic, a *shadoof*—a seesaw sort of rig with a bucket at one end and a counterbalance on the other.

Hinkel has been working on another pyramid that had been reduced to a huge pile of rubble. Under the heap lay evidence of foundation trenches, so he was able to determine the dimensions of the original base. He also found blocks that indicated the pyramid's angle of inclination. With such scant clues and massive patience, he has sorted through the rubble, numbering each block according to layer and face. Sometimes the pyramids are too far gone to rebuild; but Friedrich Hinkel has set himself the task of accounting for every loose block at the site.

He has also labored over the offertory chapels attached to the pyramids. Gradually he has pieced together the fragments of bas-reliefs that embellished the interior walls with processions of gods and royalty in full regalia. "It's like working on giant jigsaw puzzles with some parts gone forever," he said.

As in Egypt, only royalty and the rich had the means to mummify a body and preserve it; but even commoners were buried with so many possessions that scholars have concluded that a cult of the dead dominated the religious life of all Meroë.

While the Meroitic elite sought eternal life Egyptian style, they relaxed Roman fashion in the luxury of an ornate bathhouse. Yet no one would ever mistake the plastered brick building with its pool as the work of a Roman architect, for the Meroites typically altered what they borrowed to suit themselves.

By the time we drove the 2½ miles from the cemetery to the Roman Bath within the royal precincts of Meroë, the sun hovered near the edge of the world, flooding the pale desert with color. Mounds of small, black clumps of iron slag lay all about the plain at the edge of the city, gleaming darkly in the soft pink light.

Some scholars have perceived iron as the basis of Meroë's prosperity. Early in this century, English philologist A. H. Sayce decided the city "must have

PRECEDING PAGES: *Large earthen jars lashed to the ox-driven saqia, or waterwheel, raise water from the Nile for irrigation. Four families share in its operation, working 12-hour shifts during the dry season.*

Nomadic herdsmen on their way to market at Shendi pass the village of Kabushiya. Similar communities have existed since the time of the Kushite kings. But because of the impermanent nature of mud bricks, archaeologists have found only traces of the houses of that period.

been the Birmingham of ancient Africa; the smoke of its iron smelting furnaces . . . continually going up to heaven, and the whole of northern Africa might have been supplied by it with implements of iron."

More recently, Peter L. Shinnie of the University of Calgary in Alberta, Canada, excavated numerous clay furnaces and parts of bellows, proving that Meroë was indeed an iron manufacturing center, though perhaps not on the scale Sayce visualized.

Professor Shinnie, who has labored in the Sudan

for more than three decades, has also discovered great numbers of ancient cattle bones at Meroë. The finds attest to the importance of herding and bear witness to a once better climate, for it is impossible now to imagine large herds sustaining themselves on the stubble of yellow grasses on that parched plain. Professor Shinnie finds further evidence that the climate has changed in the *hafirs*, reservoirs built to catch rain and the runoff from ephemeral streams. He has detected the remains of nearly fifty of these earthen structures. "If they were building hafirs, it means they had something to catch. And it wouldn't take much rain to transform the Butana into a grassland."

After so many years as an archaeologist in the Sudan, Professor Shinnie feels he knows the Meroites.

"The Ja'aliyin, who live in the villages along the Nile north of Khartoum, have changed their religion to Islam and their language to Arabic, but without a doubt they are the direct descendants of the ancient population of Meroë," he said. "In every sculpture of a

Every Monday and Thursday the marketplace at Shendi draws crowds of farmers from surrounding villages. During the late Middle Ages, Shendi served as a primary center of the Sudan caravan trade. The market offered exotic commodities from Europe and India as well as African specialties such as the wooden dishes of Shendi blackened and hardened by fire. The bargaining over price that pertained then still prevails. Below, farmers using simple hand tools prepare a plot for a new planting of sorghum.

Meroitic king, I can see the likeness of the Ja'aliyin."

Osman el Awad, the guard who ushered me through the ruins of Meroë, had the finely chiseled features and burnished complexion of the Ja'aliyin. I decided, however, that his ancestors had not inhabited the huge palace compound, whose glory had dwindled to crumbling brick walls; I preferred to think Osman's grave manner and guarded smile identified him as a descendant of the shaven-headed priests in the Temple of Amun. Of course, not one of those priests would ever have permitted me beyond the pillared hall unless I had been a person of great importance. The small sanctuary at the end of the hall was a holy-of-holies, the dwelling place of the god, where his statue was washed, anointed, clothed, and adorned with jewels.

In Meroitic times I would have walked along a ceremonial way lined with five other temples, plastered and painted with bright colors and ornamented with gold. The glitter has all flaked away, except for traces found by Peter Shinnie and his staff, and it takes a trained eye to discern the floor plan of the temple in the eroded pillars and the walls now all but vanished.

But it took little effort to visualize the past in the village of Taragma, where women still draw water from a well and men still grow onions, millet, and sorghum on tiny plots irrigated by water lifted from the Nile by a *saqia*, or waterwheel. From a distance, across a green checkerboard of fields crisscrossed with irrigation canals, I could hear the creaking of the wooden saqia. On the bank above the river, oxen plodding in a circle turned a horizontal wheel with crude cogs that geared into a vertical wheel large enough to reach down to the Nile. Big pottery jars lashed to the rim filled with water as the turning wheel dipped them, one by one, into the river. As the wheel carried the jars back to the top, they tipped and spilled their contents into channels that ran to fields extending a hundred yards or more into the desert.

Archaeologists have found countless potsherds with the telltale knob of the jar used only on saqias. And in the villages, potters like Mohammed Salih still fashion jars that closely resemble those used in Nubia 1,900 years ago. Only Mohammed's tennis shoes added a contemporary touch.

From Taragma, just south of Meroë, it is less than two hours by Land Rover across the Butana to Musawwarat es-Sufra, site of the Great Enclosure. Whatever mysterious purpose the great complex served, Musawwarat was clearly a place where people came only to visit, for no Meroitic grave has ever been found in the vicinity.

I had to contend with the profound silence and utter desolation of the place as I tried to imagine the streams of visitors and the oft-repeated dramas of the past—the lively sounds of vendors hawking amulets or souvenirs, the greetings, the excitement, the good-natured bantering I had witnessed in the markets of Khartoum and Shendi.

Evidence of the throngs is found in the graffiti on the smooth sandstone walls of the enclosure. Visitors must have left such markings by the thousand, but only the seven hundred or so that penetrated the plaster coating and scratched the stone surface survive. In addition to drawings of giraffes, horses, cows, and camels, there are representations of Apedemak, the great lion deity of the Meroites and their god of war.

"Apedemak belongs to a tradition that is completely un-Egyptian; the Meroites continued to worship their own gods side by side with the imported ones," explained German archaeologist Fritz Hintze.

Originally an Egyptologist, Dr. Hintze went to the Sudan because he was attracted by the art and challenged by the undeciphered Meroitic language.

Until the third century B.C., the Meroites wrote their inscriptions in Egyptian hieroglyphs; then they developed their own writing system with 23 characters —far simpler than the complicated, unwieldy pictorial symbols of Egypt. But Meroitic, a language not clearly related to anything spoken today, has continued to defeat the efforts of determined scholars like Dr. Hintze and his wife, Ursula, and only the inscriptions using Egyptian hieroglyphs give some insight into the character of the people.

"The writing reveals a highly pragmatic, logical mentality," Dr. Hintze told me as we talked in his apartment in East Berlin. "For example, an Egyptian inscription will attribute a high flood of the Nile to the gods. A Meroitic one, on the other hand, will explain it as the result of heavy rains at the headwaters.

"In an early inscription, a king of the Napatan period announced his right to the throne by citing descent from the queen mother. And their funerary inscriptions mention the mother first. So it seems obvious that women played an important role, just as they do today in that part of the Sudan."

No one would doubt the power and authority of Queen Amanitore—not if he could see the imposing figure wrought in stone on the walls of the Apedemak Temple at Naqa, a town of temples ten miles south of Musawwarat. The reliefs preserve more than a figure of "a truly mountainous royal lady," as she has been described. They show a resolute warrior wielding a sword, a conqueror with prisoners at her feet, a monarch wearing a crown with the royal emblem of the cobra. It isn't hard to imagine the populace prostrating themselves before her.

According to Strabo, the Greek geographer writing about 7 B.C., another woman ruler whom he called "Candace" led the Meroitic army in a raid against

Roman troops in Egypt. We now know Candace was not a name, but a title for queen or queen mother.

Little remains of Naqa, once a thriving city with all the riches and vitality of a religious center. Near the Apedemak Temple a kiosk with rounded Roman arches and graceful pillars looks painfully out of place in the bleak desert, its purpose lost in antiquity. The god Amun also has his sanctuary, but it stands silent and empty. There are at least four other temples, but they have decayed into blocks and broken pillars, and time has swallowed their identity.

Nearby, a group of seminomadic Shaiqiya had camped beside a deep well to draw water for their

Undaunted by the camera, a mother and child of the Ja'aliyin—the people who live along the Nile for about 500 miles north of Khartoum—pause for a portrait. Over the centuries their language, religion, and political allegiance have changed, but the Ja'aliyin still show the distinctive features of their Kushite ancestors.

*A*lthough the violent gusts of a sudden sandstorm blur the afternoon sun, life's normal routines continue. Only their tin cans and galvanized pails hint of modern times as these Ja'aliyin women draw water from a village well. In the background loom round thatched shelters constructed near the fields for the temporary storage of crops.

herds of cattle and goats. Instead of multitudes coming to worship, a few families were filling goatskin bags with water, and a woman was washing clothes, slapping robe after robe against a rock. Instead of the sound of drums and the chanting of hymns, there was only the lowing of cows. Instead of a king in a chariot, a child bounced along on a donkey.

Why, I wondered, were the cities of Meroë abandoned so completely, so totally forgotten? What catastrophes consigned the civilization to such oblivion?

Many have speculated on the reasons for Meroë's fall. Professor William Y. Adams, an articulate and energetic archaeologist from the University of Kentucky, puts a large measure of blame on the camel.

"The camel was introduced into the region probably in the first century B.C. It had the same transforming influence on the nomadic Beja that the horse had on our Plains Indians. The camel gave the Beja, who had long menaced the frontiers of Kush, more mobility, and they were able to seize control of the profitable caravan trade," he said.

"The economic decline may have been hastened by overgrazing of the land and by the progressive desiccation of the Butana. But the most serious threat

came from Axum, a kingdom that rose to power in the highlands of Ethiopia to the southeast," Professor Adams continued.

"Axum challenged Kush's monopoly of trade in the African interior. The two inevitably clashed, and Axumites, on the offensive, carried the battles into the Butana. But by the time the Axumite king Aezanas marched into Kush around A.D. 350, its monarchy apparently no longer existed. A detailed Axumite inscription makes no mention of the Meroites but does refer to the Noba, a people who were known to have harassed the Meroites from the west bank of the Nile.

"So the final downfall of the Kingdom of Kush is veiled in almost complete darkness."

Some scholars hold that the Meroite aristocracy fled to the west, taking with them their belief in divine kingship and their technology for working iron, and see Meroë as the source of civilizations in western and central Africa. But Professor Shinnie finds no convincing evidence for this theory, and points out that the smelting furnaces of ancient west Africa were quite different from those employed in Meroë.

Controversy continues as the story of Meroë unfolds. Theories are advanced, then refuted. But at last Meroë is beginning to recover its place in history.

Jebel Barkal, a sacred mountain near Napata, stands a mile from the bank of the Nile and rises 300 feet above the flat riverside plain. At the base of the mountain lie the ruins of the great Kushite Temple of Amun. Nearby, windblown sand surrounds a cluster of royal pyramids (above).

FOLLOWING PAGES: *Candace Amanirenas, with her son Prince Akinidad, directs a dawn attack on the Roman garrison at Syene, today's Aswan. The formidable leader greatly impressed classical writers, who mistook the royal title of Candace for a personal name.*

PAINTING BY DAVID BLOSSOM

*D*istinctive kiosk at Naqa combines Roman architectural style with alterations typical of Meroitic tastes—as in the detailing of doorways and decorative elements. Below, incised wall reliefs, a striking feature of surviving temples at Naqa, demonstrate the blending of Meroitic and ancient Egyptian art. Although clearly Meroitic in details of dress and body proportioning, these figures on the outer walls of the Apedemak Temple stand in characteristic Egyptian attitudes.

FOLLOWING PAGES: *Six pairs of stone rams once bordered an avenue leading to the Amun Temple at Naqa. Amun, symbolized by the ram, held special eminence as god of the kings. Naqa's temples distinguish it as one of the principal Kushite religious centers.*

Goat-herding nomads visit the well at Naqa every second day. The 150-foot depth of the well requires the use of donkeys to draw the water. Transient pastoralists like these probably contributed to the Kushite civilization: Cattle bones discovered in excavations and milking scenes depicted on ancient bowls indicate that meat and milk constituted substantial parts of the Meroites' diet.

PAGES 180-181: *Silhouetted against Lake Nasser, a lone visitor stands amid the ruins of the late Meroitic period at Qasr Ibrim. Communities of at least five distinct cultures have occupied this spot: Egyptians preceded the Meroites; Romans, Nubian Christians, and Arab Muslims followed. For thousands of years Qasr Ibrim sat atop a 200-foot cliff overlooking the River Nile. In the mid-1970s the site became an island as the waters rose behind the Aswan High Dam.*

By LOUIS DE LA HABA

THE ANCIENT KHMER

"They were the masters of their world. It was quite wonderful. There was peace and order. Temples full of riches. Happy Brahmans full of good rice, good food. And, of course, some of the most magnificent temples ever built. Nothing in that part of the world could compare. Nothing! That's quite something, *n'est-ce pas?* —isn't it?"

In his apartment on a quiet Parisian cul-de-sac, archaeologist Bernard Philippe Groslier was telling me about the ancient Khmer of Cambodia, whose civilization flowered at Angkor in a jungle-covered river delta of Southeast Asia between the 9th and 14th centuries of the Christian era. Surrounded by handsome wooden cabinets full of books and notebooks, files, photographs and plans—the product of years of labor—Professor Groslier discussed the genius of the Khmer, a restless creativity that left scattered over thousands of square miles of tropical forest some of the finest sculpture and architecture ever produced.

He spoke admiringly of the people whose history and accomplishments had claimed his professional attention during most of his working life. But behind the enthusiasm of his words there flowed an undercurrent of sadness, of nostalgia. Understandably, I thought; for his lifetime endeavor came to an abrupt and irrevocable end in 1975 when the Khmer Rouge, the Communist Red Khmer, took over in Cambodia— renamed Kampuchea—to be followed in 1978 by a rival Communist invasion from neighboring Vietnam. Professor Groslier and the other French scholars who for years had been studying and restoring the ancient Khmer capital of Angkor were forced to leave the country. The painstaking work of decades was abandoned, the finely honed organization that made the work possible was dismantled, and thousands of files, plans, card indexes, and 16,000 photographic negatives were destroyed by the Communists.

Instead of the peace and order of the ancient time to which Professor Groslier alluded, grinding oppression and warfare now plagued the land and forced refugees to leave by the scores of thousands. Instead of the plentiful rice of former days, there was widespread famine that shocked the world with a death toll that reached into the millions. Vietnamese troops occupied the Angkor area and scratched graffiti on the crumbling ruins. They made their headquarters at the *Conservation*, the compound where an archaeological team had lived and worked for years under the auspices of the Royal Cambodian Government and the École Française d'Extrême-Orient. Now, in faraway Paris, Professor Groslier could only ponder the fate of all he had left behind.

"In 1975, we had about 800 Cambodian workers, 15 Frenchmen, several Cambodian students, dozens of jeeps, cranes, and bulldozers. We generated our own electricity. We made our own concrete. And we had an enormous apparatus for cutting sandstone with special saws made of diamond-steel thread. We had files, card indexes, and photographs of every square centimeter of temple and sculpture and bas-relief. Fortunately, we have duplicates of these records here in Paris, but the originals are all lost.

"Of our Cambodian students, only one is left that I know of. He is now the curator at Angkor. But he is alone. Of our 800 workers, I know of only about 50 who survived the fighting and famine. In one of the largest buildings of the *Conservation* I left—if I remember correctly—more than 6,000 statues and works of art. Apparently they are still there. But I say apparently, because we would have to go there to be certain.

"At the National Museum in the capital at Phnom Penh, where the best statuary and all the most precious pieces had been sent, the situation is the same. The museum is intact, but the important pieces— bronzes and other small objects that we had packed into crates—well, I've heard that the crates are there, but they would have to be checked one by one."

Surprisingly, Professor Groslier expressed little concern about the temples and other structures at Angkor. He believes that reports of damage resulting from the fighting in the area have been exaggerated. The buildings are so massive that they could absorb tremendous punishment — and have, over the centuries. The bullet holes, shrapnel scars, and graffiti, Professor Groslier thinks, will simply become—to future archaeologists — another part of the long and complex history of Angkor. As for the nearer future?

"Ah! Now, if this situation goes on for years and years, then there will be trouble, *n'est-ce pas?* No doubt about it. Every year something happens. A big tree dies and falls on some structure. Stones fall off during the rainy season. As long as we were there, we could do something. Now, who knows?

"But even if tomorrow you were to tell me, 'OK, let's go to Angkor; here's a check for twenty million dollars,' I could do nothing. Nothing. It would take me at least five years of full peacetime to get going again. It is a little like heart surgery. For heart surgery you need not only the surgeon, but a whole complex organization—assistants, equipment, air conditioning, support

Images of the Buddha line one of the hallowed cloisters of the great temple called Angkor Wat, originally a Hindu sanctuary. Collected by the faithful from other shrines, the statues represent many different historical periods.

PRECEDING PAGES: *Entangled in choking roots, the ruins of Ta Prohm, part of the old Khmer capital of Angkor, still stand after six centuries of the Cambodian forest's incursions. Built by Jayavarman VII, one of the greatest Khmer rulers, the temple once held priceless golden treasures.*

PRECEDING PAGES AND OPPOSITE: WILBUR E. GARRETT

systems. At Angkor, the support systems are gone."

And so the lovely monuments of Angkor—the temples, the smiling ladies carved in sandstone, the ornate lintels, the lotus towers that rise above the forest canopy, the stately colonnades—all have been left to the green grasp of the encroaching jungle. It is as if the years had rolled back to A.D. 1432, when conquering Thai armies forced the Khmer to abandon their capital. Then it lay forgotten for more than four centuries, the home of silent bats and chattering monkeys, prowling tigers, creeping forest creatures, and a few saffron-robed bonzes, Buddhist monks.

Although known to a few European travelers, Angkor was not "discovered" for the western world until a Frenchman named Henri Mouhot visited the site in 1860. Mouhot could hardly believe his eyes. In a diary later published in France, he wrote of "ruins of such grandeur, remains of structures that must have been raised at such an immense cost of labor, that, at the first view, one is filled with profound admiration. . . . One of these temples—a rival to that of Solomon, and erected by some ancient Michael Angelo—might take an honorable place beside our most beautiful buildings. It is grander than anything left to us by Greece and Rome, and presents a sad contrast to the state of barbarism in which the nation is now plunged."

In words that might well have been written for our own troubled time, Mouhot continued: "Unluckily, the scourge of war, aided by time, the great destroyer, who respects nothing . . . has fallen heavily on the greater part of the . . . monuments; and the work of destruction and decay continues among those that still remain standing."

To Mouhot, those "prodigious works" were nothing short of astounding. To Professor Groslier, the "highest architectural achievements in all Asia" are an intimate part of life, as familiar as old and cherished friends, for he grew up among them. He was born in Cambodia, as was his father, Georges Groslier, who was the first child born to French parents in what was then, in 1887, a French protectorate.

As a child Bernard Groslier visited Angkor with his father, sometimes during the rainy season when, because of flooding and lack of roads, elephants were the only means of transport. But he has little fondness for the lumbering beasts.

"Elephants make you seasick," he reminisced. "They are very slow, and they sway! You have to stop one day out of two to let them rest. They have to bathe constantly and they catch cold very easily. When you are on top of an elephant and he sneezes. . . . Oh! It is very unpleasant.

"Still, there is one thing worse than traveling by

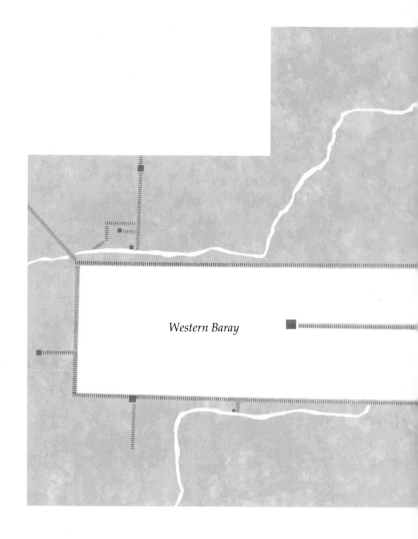

Western Baray

elephant, and that is riding in an oxcart. Of course, in my generation, when we worked at Angkor, we had jeeps. But, you know, it was with elephants and oxcarts that Angkor was built. For a long time we were puzzled by the immense amount of work involved in transporting stones from the quarries to Angkor. But after some study we concluded that all the stone needed to build Angkor Wat could have been transported by 3,000 oxcarts in five years."

Of course Angkor Wat, the great temple erected in the early 12th century by King Suryavarman II, was not built in five years. And it took closer to four centuries for all the major temples in the Angkor area to be constructed. As for the Khmer civilization itself, its roots reach to the beginning of the Christian era.

This was the time of the great Indian expansion, when seafaring merchants fanned out across the Indian Ocean and brought to Southeast Asia a seething ferment of new ideas. From Burma to Indonesia, they established a chain of settlements along the coasts from which they traded for gold, precious stones, perfumes, and spices that often found their way westward to the Roman Empire. The merchants brought with them their religions, Hinduism and Buddhism; their literary language, Sanskrit; their art and technology; their science and mathematics.

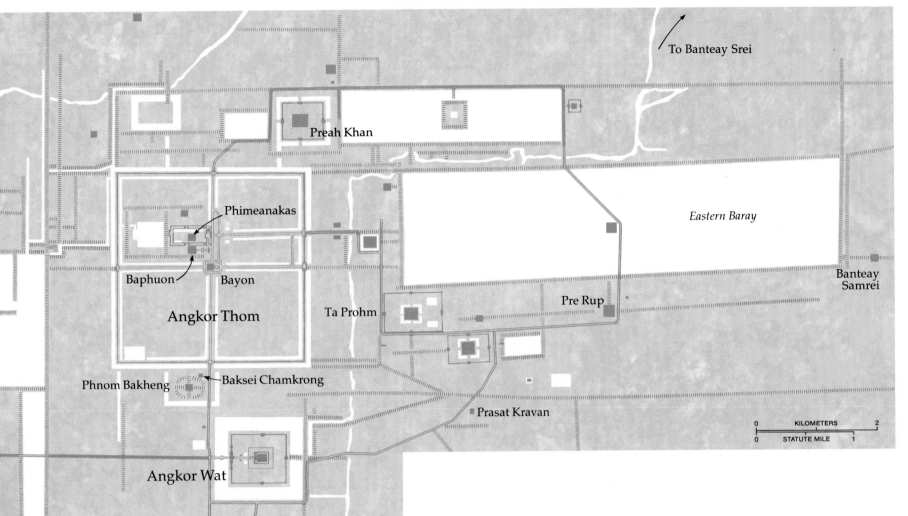

To Banteay Srei

Preah Khan

Phimeanakas

Eastern Baray

Baphuon   Bayon

Angkor Thom

Banteay
Samrei

Ta Prohm

Pre Rup

Phnom Bakheng   Baksei Chamkrong

Prasat Kravan

KILOMETERS   2

STATUTE MILE   1

Angkor Wat

*From their seat at Angkor in Cambodia, today's
Kampuchea, Khmer kings gained control of much of
Southeast Asia. In orderly magnificence, the capital
unfurled its artistic splendor with the growth of
empire. Huge artificial ponds, or barays, held water
that became in the dry season the city's life blood.
First construction began late in the ninth century A.D.;
the last, including Jayavarman VII's Bayon and the
Royal Terraces, took place between 1181 and 1220.*

PLAN OF ANGKOR BASED ON A MAP BY GUY NAFILYAN,
ÉCOLE FRANÇAISE D'EXTRÊME-ORIENT

FOLLOWING PAGES: *Lotus-spired Angkor Wat rises like
a mirrored mirage above the waters of its moat. Built
by Suryavarman II in the first half of the 12th century,
Angkor reflects classic Khmer temple architecture: Its
central tower symbolizes sacred Mount Meru, the
surrounding spires chains of mountains, the encircling
moat the mythical oceans.*

FOLLOWING PAGES: HERBERT LANKS/SHOSTAL ASSOCIATES

CHINA

VIETNAM

BURMA

•Hanoi

LAOS

•Vientiane

THAILAND

Mekong

Bangkok•
Battambang•   □ ANGKOR
                Tonle Sap

KAMPUCHEA

Phnom Penh•

*Gulf of
Thailand*

*South
China
Sea*

MALAYSIA

•Kuala Lumpur

KILOMETERS   500
STATUTE MILES   300

It would be difficult to overestimate the influence India brought to bear on the native cultures of Southeast Asia and on the civilizations that evolved there over the next millennium. As Professor Groslier wrote in *Angkor, Art and Civilization*, "The expansion of India towards the countries of the East, at the very moment when by a striking coincidence China seemed to be moving southwards to encounter it, constitutes one of the turning-points of history, paralleled only by the expansion of Greece or Rome."

The assimilation of Indian culture took different forms in different places — in Ceylon, in Burma, in Java. In Cambodia, the earliest state born of this association was the Kingdom of Funan, centered in the Mekong River delta. The Funanese soon transformed the brackish delta swamplands into rich rice-growing country. A network of canals drained the land and desalinized it with fresh water. Other canals, some of them large enough to accommodate seagoing ships, linked densely populated cities that became important overseas trading centers of India.

Little remains of Funanese art and architecture,

ABOVE: M. SERRAILLIER/RAPHO; BELOW: SIPA PRESS

though what has been found clearly shows the Indian impact. Toward the end of the Funanese preeminence —about the middle of the sixth century—Professor Groslier detects in the sculpture a "sensitive modelling" and a "clarity of line and harmony of composition that indicate the growth of a new art." In broader terms, it would appear that a distinct and creative local culture was by then emerging, stimulated by the leavening influence of India.

The Indian religions, both Hinduism and Buddhism, also flourished in this new ground. And, in an adaptation of the Hinduism of the high-caste Brahmans, there developed the concept of a supreme monarch, of an earthly king who was identified with Shiva, one of the highest of the Hindu gods, and who ruled over his people as Shiva ruled over the lesser deities. This idea, to be strengthened and refined by the Khmer, would become the motive force of their empire and, some have suggested, the reason for its eventual downfall.

To the north of Funan, and contemporary with it, the vassal state of Chenla, home of the Khmer predecessors called Mon-Khmer, was growing in power. About A.D. 550, King Bhavavarman of Chenla, actually a scion of the royal house of Funan who had married the heiress to the Chenla crown, forcibly annexed Funan and founded the Kingdom of Khmer.

His chariot drawn by prancing horses, the sun god Surya (opposite) rides the sky above a chorus of worshipers. In his right hand he holds a sacred lotus blossom. The bas-relief at Angkor Wat belongs to a larger composition depicting a heavenly sequence that includes the moon and planets. Another relief shows the Hindu conceptions of heaven and hell: At top, one of the blessed rides a luxurious litter to the rewards of a meritorious life; below, unimaginable horrors inflicted by men and beasts beset the sinful and unjust.

191

In the next two centuries this domain suffered various upheavals, including being split into several small kingdoms and coming under the domination of neighboring powers. Finally, near the end of the eighth century, the Khmer prince who was to become Jayavarman II emerged to unify the country. In A.D. 802, he proclaimed his independence and had himself anointed King of Kambuja, the name from which Cambodia and the current Kampuchea are derived. Jayavarman (all Khmer kings' names carried the suffix -*varman*, meaning "armor" or "shield") established the first Khmer capital in the Angkor area near the northern shore of the Tonle Sap, the great lake. Thus, after eight centuries of gestation, was born the civilization of the remarkable Khmer.

Professor Groslier likens this period of Khmer history to contemporary events in Europe. "Caesar conquered Gaul in 55 B.C.," he said, "and Charlemagne was crowned emperor of western Europe in A.D. 800. So, between the Roman Conquest and Charlemagne you have the full assimilation of Roman culture, a re-creation of Roman culture by France—by our ancestors—and the creation of French civilization. It was the same with Angkor: The first Indian traders arrived around the year 1 B.C. and the first Angkor king was anointed in A.D. 802—almost exactly the same time span.

"The Khmer took everything from India, from irrigation to astronomy and including Shiva and the rest of Hindu religion—just as we Gauls took everything from Rome, from engineering to Christianity. But it was we who built the great cathedrals in Paris and Chartres. And the Khmer built Angkor. Nothing in India can compare with it. Nothing."

The choice of Angkor as the site of the Khmer capital stemmed from several factors. First, it was near the geographical center of the kingdom. Second, the Tonle Sap, the great lake with its outlet to the riverine network of the Mekong, provided excellent communications with the outside world. Finally, there was the great lake itself.

"The *grand lac,* the lake, you know, is a very rare geographical phenomenon," Professor Groslier said. "In the summer, when you have the melting of snow in Tibet and the beginning of the monsoon rains, the Mekong carries so much water that some of it backs up into the Tonle Sap, which expands to ten times its normal area. By November or December, the Mekong slows down and the water again flows out of the lake. Thus you have the lake going up and down, up and down, expanding and contracting. Every year this brings fresh deposits of fertile silt to the lands along the shore, especially in the north. It is the best possible land for growing rice.

Subtle, stylized movements of modern Cambodian dancers echo the graceful poses of three apsaras, celestial dancers, in an ancient bas-relief. The art of dance delighted Khmer royalty and their subjects, as evidenced by the thousands of smiling apsaras that decorate many of the Angkor monuments.

BOTH BY WILBUR E. GARRETT

*S*tony faces guard the Gate of the
Dead, one of four main entrances
to the 12th-century Angkor Thom.
At the end of a causeway flanked by
54 giant figures tugging on a naga,
or sacred serpent, the gate leads
to the temple-city's inner precinct.
Archaeologists recovered the three-
faced, lotus-crowned sculpture
below, perhaps representing the
Buddha, from within the gate.

LEFT: BRUNO BARBEY/MAGNUM; BELOW: VICTOR R. BOSWELL, JR.
HEIGHT OF THREE-FACED HEAD APPROXIMATELY 24 INCHES

Buddhist faithful offer candles and incense sticks during a sacred ceremony in an ancient temple at Angkor. Opposite, kneeling in reverence, a Khmer monarch pays homage to the Hindu god Shiva while his personal chaplain pours an offering of melted ghee, or clarified butter, over a stone lingam. *The* lingam *symbolized Shiva as the source and creator of all life, and, as the central point of the king's capital, it enhanced his authority as well.*

OPPOSITE: PAINTING BY LLOYD K. TOWNSEND

"There is another phenomenon with the fishes of the Tonle Sap. On the south shore there are trees of a special type that grow in the water and can stand being flooded clear up to the first branches. Fish swim up the Mekong and into the Tonle Sap to lay their eggs in these branches.

"When the eggs hatch, the little fish grow beautifully because they feed on the foliage. In December, when the water begins to go down, there is a very strong current in the outlet of the lake. You have only to put out nets there and you have a million tons of fish. It is the highest yield of fish by square meter of water anywhere in the world—and that includes the Grand Banks of Newfoundland."

With this great natural bounty at their disposal, the Khmer prospered from the seventh to the ninth century. But then the expansion of empire and the growth of population began to tax the available resources, and the Khmer had to do something.

The problem was that with the monsoon rains and the flooding of the Mekong, there was too much water during part of the year — between mid-June and November—and then not nearly enough during the remaining period. Despite the fertile soil, farmers could produce only one crop of rice each year. The solution lay in devising some method of storing water in time of plenty so that it could be used for irrigation during the dry season.

The Khmer created a system of canals and storage tanks. These tanks, called *barays*, were made by building up huge earthen dikes and were filled by natural flooding and by the rains. The Khmer also diverted the waters of rivers and fed them into the canal network. Everywhere there was water—in canals, in barays, in moats surrounding the temples.

"To understand Angkor," Professor Groslier told me, "you have to understand that the important thing was not the temples but the waterworks. Angkor was a hydraulic city. Water was the key. The Khmer temple —you must not take it by itself alone. It is only a chapel built on a reservoir of water, and the reservoir, the tank, is the source of life.

"The Khmer peasant knew that very well. And the Khmer kings, you know, the kings were not crowned, they were anointed. And they were anointed with what? With water from the rivers of the kingdoms that paid tribute to Angkor. The anointing symbolized the king's power over the vassal states, a power that came from those fantastic rivers like the Mekong, the Salween, the Menam [now Chao Phraya]."

The temples were also mausoleums, holding the ashes of the kings who built them. As each new king came to power, he erected his own temple, but before he did that, he first built the waterworks associated with it—the moats and canals that linked it with the rest of the city.

To Professor Groslier, writing in *Angkor, Art and Civilization*, the city "with its walls and moats represents the world surrounded by its chain of mountains and by the mythical oceans. The temple in the center symbolizes Mount Meru, its five towers standing up like the five peaks of the sacred mountain, its terraces rising in tiers like the series of worlds. It was a ritual compass, defining by its horizontal and vertical axes the four cardinal points, the zenith, and the nadir. Its subordinate shrines represent the constellations in their courses."

In the temples were kept the stone *linga*, the symbols of the creative potency of Shiva erected by a king upon his accession to the throne. This power came to the king through the mediation of Brahman priests, an

elite group who could interpret the sacred books, make astronomical observations and calculations, and write inscriptions. Professor Groslier pointed out that they even had the authority to legitimize questionable claims to the throne by concocting elaborate, though largely bogus, genealogies. He told me of one Brahman cleric who declared the legitimacy of four usurpers in a row. Usurpers were far from rare, and, in Professor Groslier's view, because of their fresh outlook and energy often were among the most successful of Khmer rulers.

Both materially and spiritually, the king held absolute power over the country. But scholars now agree that it is erroneous to speak of "god-kings," as has been done in much of the literature about Angkor.

"Of course, you can imagine that a king who was able to build Angkor Wat, which is the third or fourth largest monument in the world, a king who was master of the most powerful empire in Indochina, was indeed a bit of a god on earth—a Napoleon or a Caesar, *n'est-ce pas*? But religiously speaking, theologically speaking, no. He was not a god."

Nevertheless, the Khmer kings acted as if they were gods, building monuments to aggrandize themselves and surrounding themselves with opulence and pomp. There were thousands of officials high and low, wives, concubines, and dancing girls, immeasurable treasures in gold, silver, jewels, and silks, and lavish praise from the subjects. "His feet were a chaplet of lotus on the heads of all the kings; he overcame his enemies in battle," goes one inscription.

Away from the peaceful capital, war was waged constantly to subjugate vassal states and exact from them the tribute that made the Khmer king's luxurious life possible. "Obviously, a king is a greater king if he has vassal kings," Professor Groslier explained. "The king of Angkor had to be recognized as superior to all others, he had to show to everyone that he was the best, that the Khmer religion and social order were the best, and that Angkor was the center of the world."

Such "royal megalomania," as Professor Groslier has called it, through its excessive demands on the Khmer people and the weakening effects of warfare,

may have been an important factor in the eventual demise of the Khmer Empire. But until 1177, the empire continued to grow and Angkor to expand its magnificent array of temples. There were sumptuous palaces as well, but these have not survived, for only the temples were built of stone; the other buildings, the palaces as well as the houses of the peasants, were all made of perishable wood.

In 889, Yasovarman I built the first great storage tank at Angkor, the Eastern Baray, a rectangular reservoir measuring about 1 by 4 miles. Punctuated by wars, revolts, and struggles for succession, the building process continued. In 967, Rajendravarman completed the ornately beautiful temple complex of Banteay Srei some 18 miles northeast of Angkor. Toward the end of that century, Jayavarman V built the temple of Phimeanakas. In the middle of the 11th century, under Udayadityavarman II, the temple called the Baphuon and the Western Baray—even larger than the Eastern—were constructed. And in the first half of the 12th century, the fabulous Angkor Wat was created under Suryavarman II, who had extended Khmer dominion into the lands we now call Laos, Thailand, and Vietnam.

Angkor was in its full glory. It was the center of empire, collector of tribute, amasser of treasure. A Chinese diplomat assigned to Angkor in the 13th century described a scene that must have been commonplace in earlier times—that of the king emerging in procession from the royal palace. The Chinese visitor, Chou Ta-kuan, wrote:

". . . soldiers march at the head of the procession, followed by the banners and standards and the musicians. Then comes a troop of some hundreds of waiting-women in flowered robes, with flowers in their hair. . . . Then come waiting-women bearing the king's gold and silver plate and insignia. . . . Then come waiting-women bearing spears and shields. . . . And after these come carriages drawn by goats or horses, all of them ornamented with gold. . . .

"The ministers and the princes are all mounted on elephants; from far off you can see the thousands of red parasols borne before them. Next come the wives and concubines of the king. . . . Behind these comes at last the king, standing on an elephant, his precious sword in hand. The elephant's tusks are . . . sheathed in gold."

Chou Ta-kuan spent a year in Angkor and left a valuable record of life in the Khmer capital. His *Notes on the Customs of Cambodia* covers not only customs but also architecture, language, geography, natural history, economics, and more. There was at the time a lively trade with China, and Chou Ta-kuan listed imports that included gold and silver, silk, lacquered trays, porcelains, mercury, paper, sandalwood, iron pots, and copper trays. In exchange, the Khmer sent

With profound faith and rich imagination, the Hindu religion adopted by the Khmer endowed the gods with varied manifestations, human or animal, sometimes both. Amiable, horse-headed Vajimukha from Pre Rup, a temple near the East Baray at Angkor, represents one form of Vishnu, the eternal savior and protector of the world. The god of intellect and learning, also from Angkor, appears as an obese, elephant-headed Ganesha, an offspring of Shiva.

elephant tusks, rhinoceros horns, beeswax, handsomely grained *laka* wood, cardamom, resins, oils, lacquer, and kingfisher feathers.

The idea that such a fragile commodity as kingfisher feathers was an important item of trade struck a poetic chord in the English writer Osbert Sitwell, who recorded his travels in the Far East during the 1930s in his book *Escape With Me!*

"Cambodian kingfishers," Sitwell wrote, "were esteemed above all others in the Chinese market . . . and were the chief source of national income: their flashing and iridescent feathers were shipped to Canton, where they were fashioned into those glittering blue and green tiaras, worn, until recent years, by every Chinese bride. . . .

"No wonder, then, that this was a water civilization. We need no longer be surprised at the extent of the artificial lakes, the number of pools and moats and basins . . . for over all of them dipped, skimmed and flashed . . . the most exquisite kingfishers. . . . No wonder, either, that these towers and cornices tend to aspire, to take to themselves the angle and shape of wings, for on wings they were built, and out of wings they came."

*I*n Chou Ta-kuan's time, the Khmer Empire was on the wane as a historical force, but the first telling blow against it had been struck more than a century earlier when the armies of Champa invaded and sacked Angkor in 1177. Palaces and houses were burned and the temples robbed of their treasures. The country was left in a state of chaos in which it remained until 1181, when the remarkable Jayavarman VII succeeded to the Khmer monarchy.

Jayavarman repulsed the Cham invaders, chased them out of his country, and invaded theirs, looting the Cham capital of Vijaya. From then until 1220, Champa remained under Khmer control. After his successful campaign, Jayavarman set about restoring the former Khmer glory. Professor Groslier likened him to Napoleon III who, as emperor of the French from 1852 until 1870, sought to bring back the grandeur of the years of Napoleon I. Although both succeeded for a time, in neither case were the results lasting.

Jayavarman died in about 1219, an old man of perhaps 90 years. To some he was the greatest of the Khmer builders. Indeed, during his reign a frenzy of construction and reconstruction took place that included, among the most important works, the erection of the towering Bayon and the rebuilding of the complex now called Angkor Thom.

Different from other temples at Angkor, the Bayon reflects the fact that, unlike most of his predecessors, Jayavarman VII was a Buddhist. The Bayon is an enormous structure, although not quite so large as Angkor Wat. Within its central shrine, laid out in the form of a lotus flower, archaeologists found a statue of the Buddha in meditation seated on the coils of a sevenheaded *naga*, a cobra named Muchilinda, whose hood extended protectively over the Buddha's head.

Jayavarman also built other temples—Ta Prohm, Preah Khan, Ta Som, and the Royal Terraces fronting on the great square of Angkor Thom.

To Professor Groslier, however, the accomplishments of Jayavarman VII fell somewhat short of the works of his predecessors. "His monuments are large and romantic and pretty, sometimes beautiful," he told me. "But the work, the technique one sees is very careless. The strength, the spine of Khmer power and art and talent had been broken in 1177, and now it was second rate, even third rate. The Cham attack cut the

flow of energy and killed a lot of the people, and the Khmer never recovered. After Jayavarman VII, not one king built a great reservoir or dug new canals, and the people were no longer happy with their kings."

Although the Khmer monarchy reverted to Hinduism for a short period after Jayavarman VII, he had

From the Himalayas' icy heights, the stately Mekong River (below, right) courses to the South China Sea, bringing sustenance to the heart of Southeast Asia. The Kampuchean capital of Phnom Penh nestles between two tributaries, the Bassac (lower left) and Tonle Sap Rivers. Floodwaters from the mountains' spring and summer snow-melts not only enrich the river-bordering ricelands but also produce, today as in the past (relief at right), a bountiful crop of fish.

succeeded in introducing a certain outlook, a compassionate philosophy that, catching hold upon his subjects, may have contributed to their discontent with subsequent, old-style kings. Jayavarman considered himself a man of his people. For them he built 102 hospitals; on the foundations were inscribed the words: "He suffered from the ills of his subjects more than from his own; for it is the public sorrow which makes the grief of kings, and not private afflictions."

In the convention of Buddhist sculpture, Jayavarman's statues show him in a meditative posture, head slightly lowered, eyes closed, and on his lips, I thought, the hint of a smile. In his charming Gallic fashion, Professor Groslier soon set me right.

"No, he is not smiling," he lectured. "In Buddhist meditation you are liberating yourself from worldly considerations. You are not happy, you are—how would you say?—serene. You are happy if you meet the girl of your life; but if you realize that there is no girl of your life, you are serene. There is a distinction there, somewhere." And Professor Groslier smiled. Happily.

It is possible that the orgy of building under Jayavarman VII contributed to the decline of the Khmer monarch's power by its excessive demands on the people's energy and resources. More likely, only the seeds of the people's disenchantment were planted then, since obviously at the time of Chou Ta-kuan—77 years after Jayavarman's death—the pomp and panoply were still going full force. Another factor in the decline of power may have been the Buddhist religion, which was widespread among the lower classes of people—those who had little participation and even less interest in the refinements of Shivaism and the glorification of the upper classes and the king.

"People came to have less and less faith in the king," Professor Groslier said. "So the king had less and less power and less ability to wage war.

"Food may have been a factor. There were no new irrigation projects after Jayavarman, and the old canals were becoming silted up. Perhaps the soil was becoming exhausted. It is a very complex picture.

"I think, too, that they died of too much glory. I think they died of exhaustion and just quit. Just like Rome. There are those who say Rome was destroyed by barbarians, and those who say Rome destroyed herself because she no longer believed in her sense of right and wrong."

Angkor's destruction is not well documented. We know that after Jayavarman VII, the empire began to shrink with the loss of control over neighboring vassal states and the rise of Thai power to the west. The city appears to have been captured by Thai armies on several occasions, the last in 1432, when a final attack took place that caused its permanent abandonment and the moving of the capital to the present location at Phnom Penh.

Before leaving Paris and the pleasant and instructive company of Professor Groslier, I sought out Mlle Madeleine Giteau, former curator of the Cambodian National Museum at Phnom Penh and of the two now-destroyed museums at Battambang. I was lucky to find her at home in August, a time when many Parisians prefer to leave their capital to hosts of invading tourists.

A leading authority on Khmer art and iconography, Mademoiselle Giteau has published both scholarly and popular works on the subject. Together we leafed through some of her books as we talked about the Khmer. It was she who told me about Muchilinda, the naga with the euphonious name who protected the meditating Buddha from the falling rain.

She had seen a recent photograph taken inside the National Museum, and was encouraged to see that everything appeared much as she had left it in 1975 when she was compelled to depart by the arrival of the Khmer Rouge. But she was less hopeful about the smaller pieces, the ones that had been left packed in storage. These, she felt, had probably been stolen and sold.

It turned out Mademoiselle Giteau is an admirer of Jayavarman VII. "Oh, yes!" she said. "I knew him very well. I passed his statue in the museum every day on the way to my office. I like him very much."

Jayavarman rebuilt and expanded Angkor in the hope that it would last "for as long as the sun and the moon shall endure," that is, during our *kalpa*, a cosmic period of more than four billion years that is supposed to represent a day and a night in the life of the Hindu god Brahma.

Mademoiselle Giteau, who, like Professor Groslier, has been intimately involved with the splendors of Khmer culture and who, like him, has been forced to give up the work of a lifetime, shares Jayavarman's hope. As she wrote in the final paragraph of her book *The Civilization of Angkor:*

"For as long as the Khmer monuments remain standing, even ruined as they are, and the divine images remain absorbed in their blissful meditations, Khmer civilization will not perish. May the prayer of Jayavarman VII be thus granted, and this testimony of Khmer civilization survive until the end of the time of our kalpa."

Under the luminous glow of a full winter moon, a Khmer fisherman gracefully tosses his net into the teeming Tonle Sap. Before the lake's waters begin to recede, a simple cast brings a sagging netful of carp and other fish grown fat from a summer's browsing amid the submerged vegetation.

Torested in stone, the temple-mountain known as the Bayon raises clifflike walls and towers against a cloud-paled sky. French archaeologist Bernard Philippe Groslier, long-time excavator and restorer of Khmer ruins, has called this massive structure "the most amazing piece of architecture in existence." Colossal faces on each of the Bayon's 54 secondary towers gaze impassively toward the distant horizon. The central spire tops a sanctuary that once sheltered an image of the Buddha. King Jayavarman VII, builder of the Bayon and the surrounding Angkor Thom, or Great Temple, actively fostered the Buddhist faith after ascending the Khmer throne in 1181. During his reign, a frenzy of building activity took place in the Khmer capital, bringing to Angkor a new and less formal, more humanistic style of art. Because of the hasty construction, however, quality declined, and Jayavarman VII's temples have suffered more extensive deterioration than many of the earlier monuments.

WILBUR E. GARRETT

205

*L*ost in Buddhist contemplation, Jayavarman VII gazes inwardly, a half-smile of serenity on his lips. To some, Jayavarman ranked as the greatest of Khmer rulers—a decisive and victorious general, a tireless builder of monuments and empire, above all a monarch whose compassion and humanity brought a new dimension to Khmer life. On the foundations of the many hospitals he built, stone carvers inscribed his exemplary words: ". . . it is the public sorrow which makes the grief of kings, and not private afflictions." Jayavarman rose to power relatively late in life, at about 50 or 55, and at a time when the Khmer kingdom lay in shambles, its capital ransacked and burned by neighboring Champa. Under his command a great army of archers, spearmen, and elephants set out to avenge the defeat. Before the war of conquest ended, Jayavarman had extended his dominion over most of Southeast Asia. Bas-reliefs at the Bayon, below, commemorate the battles against Champa.

PAGES 208-209: PAINTING BY DAVID BLOSSOM: BELOW: MADELEINE GITEAU

*P*olo players charge the ball on spirited mounts (PRECEDING PAGES) under the eye of King Jayavarman VII, seated beneath a parasol on the royal Elephant Terrace at Angkor Thom. The popular sport, also depicted in the relief above, sometimes matched commoners against noblemen, according to accounts from nearby Thailand; a victory by the commoners during New Year festivities signaled a prosperous year ahead for all the Khmer people. Carved on the 400-yard-long wall of the terrace (top and right), a parade of elephants marches through the forest in a series of scenes that include tiger, wild ox, and deer hunts.

Terrace of the Leper King (right), one of the last monuments built under Jayavarman VII late in the 12th century, acquired its name from a probably incorrect belief that Jayavarman suffered from leprosy. Restoring the outer wall, archaeologists found a wall behind it—perhaps an earlier phase of construction, or a work covered up because the demons sculptured on it represented the underworld.

*M*asterwork of Khmer architecture, the graceful temple of
Banteay Srei appears as an almost hidden jewel in its remote
forest setting. More a miniature than a full-size shrine, its tallest
tower rises only 33 feet, unlike the massive pyramids elsewhere
in the Khmer region. Construction of the exquisite pink sandstone

complex, a group of buildings that included sanctuaries, libraries, and monastic quarters, ended in A.D. 967, when the Brahman priest Yajnavaraha dedicated it to Shiva. Students of Khmer art consider the Banteay Srei a summation of the best artistic traditions that preceded it and a departure from the monolithic style of the past. The lavishly decorated monument, 18 miles northeast of Angkor, has earned the name Citadel of the Women because of its many female sculptures and also, perhaps, because of its dainty ornamentation.

*A*mid a profusion of filigree-like carvings, grotesque seated figures with heads of monkeys, parrots, and tigers guard the entrances to Banteay Srei's shrines. Three-tiered pediments surmount the doorways of two of the libraries. Female deities like that below, carved in a flowing, naturalistic style, flank doorways of the central sanctuary.

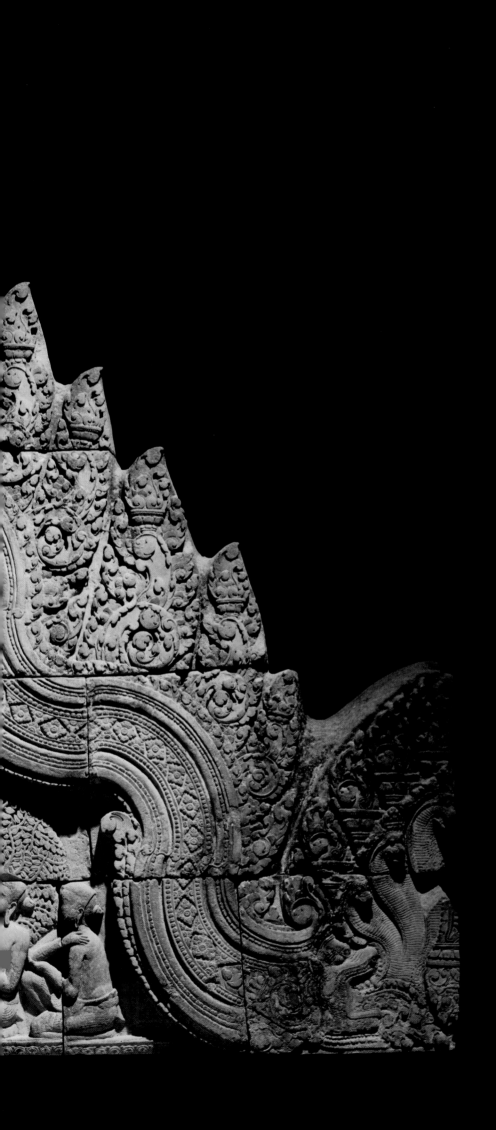

*Like a delicate flower, a finely wrought
pediment unfolds a scene of myth and motion
above a doorway at Banteay Srei. Two
brothers, Sunda and Upasunda, battle over
the heavenly dancer Tilottama while a pair
of demons flies overhead. Such mythical
scenes, brought to life by the skill of Khmer
stone carvers, made the Banteay Srei unique
among ancient Cambodian monuments.*

FOLLOWING PAGES: *Grim-faced among
the priceless monuments of Angkor, a
Vietnamese soldier stands guard against
rival Communist guerrillas of the dreaded
Khmer Rouge. War came to Angkor in
the early 1970s, when the Khmer Rouge
took over in Cambodia, changing its name
to Kampuchea; and again in 1978, when the
Vietnamese-backed Heng Samrin ousted
them. Today Vietnamese troops make their
headquarters at the same site where French
archaeologists formerly made theirs. Reports
abound of looting, damage by shells and
shrapnel, and desecration by graffiti-writing
soldiers. But Angkor has seen worse—
Champa sacked it in 1177, and Thai armies
conquered the city twice, in 1353 and 1432.
Looting of statuary and carvings has gone
on at least since the site was "discovered"
by the Frenchman Henri Mouhot in 1860.
Still, Angkor endures; and those who have
spent lifetimes studying its treasures voice
hope that it will continue to do so despite
the calamities that have befallen the
once-proud Khmer capital.*

LEFT: VICTOR R. BOSWELL, JR.;
FOLLOWING PAGES: PHILIP JONES GRIFFITHS/MAGNUM

THE HITTITES

By LOUIS DE LA HABA
Photographed by MEHMET BIBER

In the subdued lighting of a hallway in the United Nations General Assembly building in New York City, an oblong sculpture glistens metallically from its place on a wall. Carved on this copper object are rows of wedge-shaped characters in a language of unmistakable antiquity. A framed legend identifies the sculpture as a modern reproduction, on a larger scale, of a small clay tablet unearthed in 1906 near the village of Boğazköy, today called Boğazkale, on Turkey's vast Anatolian Plateau. The writing on the sculpture is Akkadian cuneiform, the diplomatic language of the ancient Near East.

As I looked at it, I could hear diplomats of several nations walking behind me along the carpeted hallway, conversing in quiet tones. These, I reminded myself, were some of the men and women whose daily work is the furtherance of mankind's latest effort to establish brotherhood and peace. Those same ideals, I knew, were expressed on the sculpture before me—a representation of a peace treaty that was negotiated more than 3,000 years ago.

"Treaty of Rea-mashesha mai Amana, the great king, the king of the land of Egypt, the valiant, with Hattusili, the great king of the land of Hatti, his brother, for establishing good peace and good brotherhood worthy of great kingship between them forever," the cuneiform text begins.

The treaty goes on to define the relationship between the two nations; to renounce aggression; to establish a defensive alliance; to guarantee, upon the death of either party, the succession of his legitimate heir; and to provide for the extradition of fugitives.

Portions of the Boğazköy tablet are missing, but the full text of the treaty is known from Egyptian hieroglyphic versions carved on a wall of the great temple at Karnak and at the Ramesseum at Thebes. One of the final passages calls upon the gods as witnesses to the good faith of the signatories:

"As for these words . . . as for him who shall not keep them, a thousand gods of the land of Hatti, together with a thousand gods of the land of Egypt, shall destroy his house, his land, and his servants."

The Boğazköy tablet, scholars have learned from the Egyptian texts, was the ancient equivalent of a "file copy" of an original tablet made of silver. "Rea-mashesha mai Amana," they know, was the Egyptian Pharaoh Ramses II—"Ramses beloved of Amun." But for a long time—long after the Egyptian hieroglyphs had been deciphered but before archaeologists had found the Boğazköy tablet—no one knew the identity of Hattusili or of his country, the land of Hatti. Who, scholars wondered, was this king who spoke as a brother of the great Egyptian pharaoh? Where was this land of Hatti? And what events culminated in a treaty that seemed so advanced even when judged by modern standards of international relationships?

Fragments of a 3,250-year-old treaty (opposite) speak eloquently of mankind's age-old quest for peace. Inscribed in Akkadian cuneiform, the international language of the ancient Near East, the treaty ended hostilities between two principal powers of the 13th century B.C.—Egypt and the Hittite Empire of Asia Minor. Above, visitors to the United Nations inspect a large copper sculpture of the clay tablet. Excavators recovered the tablet in 1906 from the ruins of Hattusa, the Hittite capital.

PAGES 220-221: *Sere and craggy landscape cradles the remains of the imperial city. Across the high ground at center spreads the Büyükkale, citadel of Hittite kings.*

Black Sea

Istanbul•

Boğazkale □ ALACAHÖYÜK
Ankara • •□ HATTUSA

TURKEY

□ KÜLTEPE

□ EFLATUN PINAR

Mediterranean Sea

SYRIA

KADESH □

| 0 | KILOMETERS | 250 |
| 0 | STATUTE MILES | 150 |

HATTUSA

Yazılıkaya

| 0 | METERS | 500 |
| 0 | FEET | 1500 |

Great Temple

Lower City

Büyükkale

Upper City

Nişantepe

Lion Gate

Yenicekale
Temples

King's Gate

Sphinx Gate

Answers to these questions have been slowly forthcoming since the early 1900s through the painstaking labor of archaeologists, epigraphists, philologists, and other scholars. Today we know that the land of Hatti was the empire of the Hittites, a people who flourished between the 17th and 12th centuries B.C., then all but disappeared from history. Not until the 19th century of our own time did their civilization again come to light.

At various moments the Hittite Empire covered much of Anatolia, or Asia Minor, and portions of northern Syria. This the Hittites accomplished both through military conquest, for they were superb fighting men, and through alliances often based on royal marriages, for they were also skilled in diplomacy.

They became one of the major powers in the Near East and vied with Egypt for supremacy in the region. A Hittite king, Mursili I, conquered Babylon and put an end to a dynasty that had included the great lawgiver Hammurabi. Another, Suppiluliuma I, was asked by the widow of the Egyptian boy-king Tutankhamun to give her one of his sons in marriage. Suppiluliuma was flabbergasted ("Such a thing has never happened to me in my whole life," he is quoted in one of the Hittite tablets). After some hesitation, he sent off his son Zannanza to the bereaved lady. But by then a new ruler had seized power, and Zannanza was murdered before reaching his destination.

Thereafter relations between the Egyptians and the Hittites worsened until, about 1286 B.C., a great battle took place on the frontier of the two empires, near a city named Kadesh on the Orontes River in Syria. It pitted the forces of King Muwatalli, grandson of Suppiluliuma, against those of Ramses II. Through a stratagem, the Hittites ambushed and nearly overwhelmed their enemy. But Egyptian reinforcements arrived in the nick of time, and the Hittite forces had to regroup within Kadesh. By next day's end the two sides had disengaged, and each claimed victory, though many scholars believe the battle was a standoff. Sixteen years later, Hattusili III, a successor of Muwatalli, signed the peace treaty with Ramses, a treaty further solemnized by the marriage of one of Hattusili's daughters to the Egyptian pharaoh.

Seeking to learn more about these nearly forgotten people whose light shone so briefly, yet so brightly, upon the ancient world, I traveled to Turkey and its heartland in the rolling steppes of central Anatolia. My quest began at Boğazkale, some 90 miles east of the

Centered near the present-day town of Boğazkale, the Hittite Empire controlled much of Anatolia and parts of Syria at its peak of power between 1400 and 1200 B.C. The story of Hattusa's site goes back considerably farther; the Hittites' predecessors occupied the lower city as early as 2300 B.C.

Turkish capital of Ankara. Boğazkale is a small agricultural town where flocks of fat geese waddle through winding streets bordered by solid, tile-roofed peasant houses. At the edge of town, a few farmers were threshing their wheat with donkey-drawn sledges and winnowing the grain by pitching it into the wind.

South of Boğazkale, the almost treeless landscape rises steeply in craggy convoluted folds that form a spur between two northward-flowing streams. On this sloping tongue of land once stood a city named Hattus, one of many independent city-states in Anatolia. Some time after 1800 B.C., a man named Anitta, king of another city, Kussara, conquered and razed Hattus. For reasons lost to history, Anitta placed a curse upon Hattus: "Whoever becomes king after me and settles this city anew, let him be smitten by the Storm God of Heaven."

Though they preserved it in their traditions, the Hittites ignored Anitta's curse, and at some time during the early 17th century B.C. established their capital on the site of old Hattus and renamed it Hattusa. The heavily fortified capital was bordered by a massive wall that in the 13th century B.C. extended for about four miles along its perimeter. Several elaborate gateways with heavy, bronze-covered wooden doors and stone archways controlled movement in and out of the city. Guard towers flanked the gates and rose at intervals along the crenellated wall. The structure was a masterwork of military architecture.

Most of the wall has been toppled by time. When I visited Hattusa, I found Turkish laborers rebuilding a section of the battlement under the watchful eye of tall, lanky Peter Neve, director of excavations at the site for the German Archaeological Institute. An architect by training and an archaeologist in practice, Dr. Neve has worked at Hattusa for more than twenty years, and took over direction of the project in 1973 from the distinguished archaeologist Professor Kurt Bittel.

When I marveled at the strength and complexity of the fortifications, Dr. Neve explained that the Hittites lived in constant fear of attack, especially from the Kaska people to the north. "They had conflicts all the time," he said, "and the Kaska were always causing trouble. During the reign of King Muwatalli, in the late 14th or early 13th century B.C., the Kaska attacked Hattusa and set it ablaze. Muwatalli fled, taking his court and the Hittite cult gods with him. After the Kaska had been brought under some measure of control, Muwatalli's son, Uri-Teshub, returned to Hattusa and restored the city as the imperial capital."

The work Dr. Neve was supervising involved nearly a third of a mile of wall at the southern, higher part of the city. At the southernmost point of the wall is the Sphinx Gate, a structure once ornamented by four stone sphinxes. Unlike the other gates, which opened to chariot roads, the Sphinx Gate was intended for pedestrians, and led to two long and steep stone stairways that slanted across an artificial earthen rampart on which the wall was built. Cutting through this man-made hill and directly beneath the gate is a curious, 76-yard-long narrow tunnel that leads from the city to a point outside the wall midway between the two great staircases.

The reason for this tunnel remains obscure. It may have been a simple entryway permitting pedestrians to avoid the climb up and down the stairs; or it may have had a religious purpose, for this part of Hattusa is full of temples. At the time of my visit, Dr. Neve was preparing to excavate a temple whose existence had not been known until 1978, even though archaeological work at the site has been going on since 1906.

Dr. Neve thinks that Hattusa, at least in the later years of the empire, was populated mostly by officials — the king and his court, religious functionaries, scribes, and artisans—and that ordinary people lived in special quarters mostly outside the city walls.

Some residential areas have been explored near the Great Temple of the Storm God of Heaven and the Sun Goddess of Arinna, and others on the road to the royal citadel; but where the bulk of the people lived and how they conducted their daily lives are questions that remain, for the most part, unanswered. The official life of the city is quite another matter, best exemplified by what has been learned from excavations at the Great Temple and the royal citadel.

This last, called the Büyükkale (Turkish for "Great Castle"), lies about midway between the upper city and the older, lower city. The Büyükkale occupies a rocky prominence on the eastern edge of Hattusa. In its day it was a fortress within a fortress, with a thick wall of its own. Its buildings bordered three courtyards. Among the structures were the king's residence and a great audience hall. The Büyükkale also had its own temple and two main libraries, where thousands of cuneiform clay tablets and fragments of tablets have been found since the early 1900s.

Building foundations of the Büyükkale were made of stone blocks and have been partially reconstructed. The long-vanished walls, formed of mud brick and wooden beams, were destroyed in a great fire in the late 13th or early 12th century B.C.

It is possible to get a feeling for the elaborate complexity of the Büyükkale from the layout of buildings and rooms. Standing in the audience hall, I could sense the ambience of its former majesty; and in one of the archive rooms I understood the thrill of discovery with which the German scholar Hugo Winckler came upon the treasure of clay tablets from which we have learned so much about Hittite culture.

In the lowest part of the city, visible from the Büyükkale, are the foundations of the Great Temple— huge blocks of granite and limestone closely fitted on their matching surfaces but otherwise roughly dressed. Construction must have been an immense task. "One of those blocks weighs more than forty tons —*forty tons!*" Dr. Neve exclaimed admiringly.

The temple had a ceremonial entryway with a central gate room and inner and outer vestibules separated by doors. Worn spots on the stone floor of the gate chamber show where the massive doors rubbed as they were opened and closed thousands upon thousands of times over the centuries. The gateway opened to an interior courtyard ending in a colonnade of granite pillars. From the colonnade, small rooms led to the inner sanctuaries, where the cult statues of the Storm God and the Sun Goddess were kept.

No such statue has ever been found, doubtless because they were made of precious metals. A tablet from one of the temple archives states that "The deity has now been made as a statue in silver covered with gold in the shape of a bull standing on all fours." The bull is an old Anatolian symbol that goes back to Neolithic times. The Storm God sometimes was represented as a bull and at other times was shown accompanied by two bulls that pulled his sacred chariot.

The sanctuaries where the cult statues were displayed were small rooms, where only a few people could be present for ceremonies—probably only the king and queen and a few temple officials and attendants. There were other ceremonies, however, that involved large groups of people and solemn processions that brought the cult statues out of their sanctuaries. One of these may have been the annual spring festival, an occasion that lasted for several weeks and included a procession along a ceremonial highway from Hattusa to a rock shrine named Yazılıkaya a little more than a mile to the northeast.

Taking part were probably the king and queen and their attendants, priests, dignitaries, musicians, and perhaps jugglers and acrobats. Oxen, goats, and sheep were likely brought along as sacrificial offerings to the gods, who would witness the dedication of the new year. Charioteers and runners must also have taken part, for the texts mention horse and foot races.

Yazılıkaya is a limestone outcropping where canyonlike clefts form two open-air galleries of unequal size. Ceremonial gateways gave access to these chambers. Few would dispute the British scholar J. G. Macqueen's description of Yazılıkaya as "the most impressive of all Hittite religious structures."

*I*n the larger of the two galleries, I felt I had entered another world. Whereas outside it had been hot and bright, here everything was shady and cool, for the chamber's walls are so steep and high that the sun's direct rays do not enter until late morning. Carved in the rock walls is a friezelike band depicting a number of deities that appear to move toward the rear of the gallery and converge at a point dominated by the Storm God and his consort, Hepatu. In all, some 65 deities are shown. Though now rather badly eroded, they are rich in detail and have provided a wealth of information about Hittite religion, symbolism, and even dress and weaponry.

It was before this divine assemblage, scholars believe, that the king and queen poured their libations of wine and made their offerings of meat and bread. Outside, other festival activities may have taken place —races, wrestling or boxing, stone-throwing contests, and similar entertainments.

Many of the deities at Yazılıkaya may be identified by symbols traditionally associated with them—the Sun God by the winged sun disk above his head, for example. Most have their names carved in hieroglyphs —quite unlike Egyptian hieroglyphs—above their upraised hands. Philologists have determined that the names of the Yazılıkaya deities are not in the Hittite language but in that of a neighboring people, the Hurrians, with whom the Hittites had considerable contact. Puduhepa, wife of Hattusili III, was a Hurrian. Although the Hittites had names of their own for the gods, they also had a habit of adopting gods, names and all, from the peoples around them, and adding them to their ever-growing pantheon. It was probably no exaggeration when "a thousand gods" were invoked as witnesses to the peace treaty with Egypt.

The second of the two galleries is believed by some scholars to be a mortuary shrine for the son of Hattusili and Puduhepa, Tudhaliya IV. Three niches are carved into the walls. One of them may once have held an urn containing Tudhaliya's ashes; his name appears twice in this chamber, once as a hieroglyph on a wall near the place where his statue may have stood, and a second time in a rock carving that ranks among the finest of Hittite compositions. This is a relief showing two figures identified by hieroglyphs. The larger is

Cloaked in the furs of winter, King Hattusili III and Queen Puduhepa lead a solemn procession from the gateway of the Great Temple. Their eldest daughter follows, accompanied by the envoy who will escort her to Egypt. The princess's marriage to Ramses II proclaimed the goodwill prevailing between Hatti and Egypt and further sealed the treaty pledges signed 13 years earlier.

PAGES 226-227: *Huge storage jars suggest the enormous wealth expended in Hittite religious activities. The jars, found embedded in the ground amid the ruins of the Great Temple complex, probably held ritual oil or wine.*

Natural limestone outcroppings form two chambers of the shrine of Yazılıkaya, site of important religious festivals. On the converging walls of the larger room (below), a rock-carved procession of some 65 deities marches toward the rear, where heroic figures of the Storm God and his wife, Hepatu, stand facing each other (detail at left).

the god Sharrumma, the smaller is Tudhaliya IV. The relief depicts Sharrumma, son of the Storm God of Heaven and the goddess Hepatu, with his arm about the shoulders of the king as if to protect him. His left hand holds Tudhaliya's hand as if to guide him. Among the Hittites, when a king died it was said that he became a god, and the relief may represent a celebration of Tudhaliya's entry into the Hittite pantheon. In any event, the scene makes a powerful emotional and political statement. Here, for all to see, is Tudhaliya embraced by his patron god. Who would dare challenge the authority of one so near to the gods? Indeed, in Hittite practice, disobedience to the king was one of the few offenses punishable by death—not just of the offender but of his family as well.

This form of collective responsibility in the relationship between a subject and the king extended to, or perhaps derived from, the relationship between a king and the gods. In the peace treaty, for example, the gods are called upon to destroy the party who violates it, and also "his house, his land, and his servants." The point also emerges in a prayer by Mursili II, a king who ruled near the end of the 14th century B.C.:

"Hattian Storm God, my lord, ye gods, my lords! It is only too true that man is sinful. My father sinned and transgressed against the word of the Hattian Storm God, my lord. But I have not sinned in any respect. It is only too true, however, that the father's sin falls upon the son. So my father's sin has fallen upon me.... Take pity on me and drive the plague out of the Hatti land!"

In the Hittite mind, the temporal and the spiritual —affairs of state and matters of religion—were inseparably intertwined. The king was also chief priest. The temples, as Dr. Neve pointed out, were not just places of worship but also played a major role in the economic life of the city. They owned property—both land and the peasants who tilled it; and they employed craftsmen, scribes, and servants.

230

Some of this became evident when I walked through the ruins of the Great Temple and saw the storehouses that surrounded the main building. Many of the rooms were once filled with objects of gold, silver, bronze, lead, and iron—the last a product just coming into use and valued more highly than gold. Other rooms contained huge clay jars embedded in the floors. These were used for storage, perhaps for grain or wine, and one of them, I was told, had a capacity of nearly 3,000 liters.

The temple, with its own scribes, kept its own records, and in its archives many more cuneiform clay tablets have been found. Among them were several containing instructions to temple officials on such matters as personal cleanliness and the safeguarding of temple property. The 13th instruction warns:

"Further: Be very careful with the matter of fire. . . . When night falls, quench well with water whatever fire remains on the hearth. . . . If he who is to quench it becomes criminally negligent . . . he who commits the crime will perish together with his descendants. . . . So for your own good be very careful in the matter of fire."

Like the law against treason, the fire law also applies the principle of collective responsibility, extending punishment beyond the transgressor to his entire family. This principle found its epitome in a law designed to protect a farmer's property. If a farmer sowed a field and then another came and plowed it over, the second man was to be put to death by stretching his limbs. But the law did not stop there; it went on to direct that the second man's oxen should also be killed, and in the same manner as their owner.

There is considerable evidence that such harsh penalties belonged to an early body of Hittite law, and that later in the second millennium B.C. some reforms were instituted and punishments became more humane. Many of the laws make statements that whereas "formerly" a certain penalty—such as death or maiming—was in force, "now" the penalty involved only restitution or the payment of a fine.

Without the information provided by such texts, our knowledge of the Hittites would be limited to inferences derived from the work of archaeologists alone. But scholars who have studied the documents have given us revealing insights into the Hittite mind.

From the tablets we have precise descriptions of various rituals: to counteract sorcery, to end pestilence, to engage the help of protective demons, to patch family quarrels, even to cure impotence. One tablet contains the words of Muwatalli, the king who fought at Kadesh, concerning what must be said to the gods "when things get too much for a man."

A leading authority on Hittite texts is Dr. Hans G. Güterbock, a philologist who worked in Turkey for many years and helped set up Ankara's splendid Museum of Ancient Anatolian Civilizations. Dr. Güterbock is now at the Oriental Institute of the University of Chicago, where I met him on my return from Turkey.

"The more you read Hittite texts, the more you get into the little things, the more human the people seem," Dr. Güterbock commented. "For instance, almost all the tablets we have are very much on the official side: annals of kings, treaties, laws, epics and myths, prayers, endless descriptions of cult festivals, and so on. So you don't often get a picture of the ordinary lives of the people. Now, there's a clay tablet from a site called Maşat, where the king is sending letters to the military commander, that shows us a different aspect. You see, these people did not themselves read or write. They used scribes, and the scribes used the occasion of these letters to add their own little personal messages. In this letter the king says to the local commander something like 'I have received your report about the approaching enemy, and don't worry, we have already ordered (Continued on page 238)

Visitors to the smaller chamber at Yazılıkaya (opposite) study an underworld deity in the form of a sword god. Next to that image, a relief of Tudhaliya IV shows him in the protective embrace of his patron god. The niche beyond may have held the dead king's ashes.

With delicate artistry, Hittite craftsmen fashioned elaborate seals (above) for stamping official and commercial documents and correspondence. The five-sided stone seal at top depicts religious scenes; the perforation through its hammer-shaped handle enabled the owner to carry the seal around his neck with a thong or cord. Hieroglyphs on the gold signet ring identify it as that of the son of a king. A plaster impression appears to the lower right of each seal.

ABOVE: VICTOR R. BOSWELL, JR.
FIVE-SIDED SEAL SHOWN SLIGHTLY SMALLER;
RING SLIGHTLY LARGER THAN ACTUAL SIZE

*S*ilver cup and a goddess in gold attest to the talent of Hittite metalsmiths. A stag at rest inspired the shape of an elegant rhyton, or drinking horn, from central Anatolia. The bas-relief frieze below the cup's lip appears at near left as a flat strip, "rolled out" by a special photographic technique. The god-protector of wildlife stands on a stag, holding a bird of prey in one hand and a curved staff in the other. Behind him another figure, probably a goddess, sits on a chair before an altar or brazier. She also holds a bird—a falcon or hawk— in one hand. Three worshipers, perhaps successful hunters giving thanks, bring offerings to the deities. Below, a goddess with disk-shaped headdress sits on a throne holding an infant on her lap.

ALL BY VICTOR R. BOSWELL, JR., AND OTIS IMBODEN
STAG CUP APPROXIMATELY 7 INCHES HIGH, GODDESS 1¾ INCHES

235

Menacing lions keep evil at bay at the outer face of one of the gates piercing Hattusa's fortress walls. The double entryway, made of great stone blocks that formed two parabolic arches, once had two sets of wooden doors covered with bronze plating. Gatekeepers closed them at night and secured them with heavy beams of wood. Stone sentry towers topped with mud-brick crenellations flanked the ten-foot-wide entrance. Above, villagers ride their donkeys through the King's Gate on Hattusa's eastern perimeter. A copy of a statue of a warrior-god, considered one of the finest examples of Hittite sculpture, guards the left side of the inner archway. The original stands in the Museum of Ancient Anatolian Civilizations in Ankara. The god wears a conical helmet and kiltlike skirt, and carries a sword and battle-ax.

the necessary things.' Period. And then the scribe adds a few words to his colleague at Maşat: 'What happened to the ox you promised me? I still have not received it.' You see, all of a sudden these people come alive. They become individuals."

Despite such illuminating details, there are huge gaps in our knowledge of the Hittites, including the most basic question of all: Just who were they?

It is known that the Hittites were not native to Anatolia. Scholars have determined this from the Hittite language, which was a branch of the Indo-European family—the same language group that includes Sanskrit, Greek, Latin, and English. The natives of the part of eastern Anatolia occupied by the Hittites were a people called Hattians—the term from which the Hittites derived the name of their country. Not much is known about the Hattic language, but it was definitely not Indo-European. Most scholars agree that the Indo-Europeans came from somewhere north of the Black Sea, but opinion is divided on whether they entered Anatolia from Europe or came from the northeast across the Caucasus. To complicate matters further, there was not just one Indo-European language spoken in Anatolia, there were three closely related ones—Hittite, in central Anatolia; Palaic, in the north; and Luwian, in the south.

Hittitologists who support the western-approach hypothesis believe the Indo-European speakers moved out of Europe during the third millennium B.C., penetrated Anatolia, then spread eastward along the south coast, and finally into the land of Hatti. Along the way the dialects became differentiated.

Those who favor a route across the Caucasus can also marshal compelling arguments. Dr. Güterbock counts himself among those who support a trans-Caucasian theory, but also believes that the division into Luwian, Palaic, and Hittite took place in Anatolia.

"The three dialects are so close that it would be stretching probability too far to assume that they split off in the original homeland and then all three happened somehow to end up in Anatolia," he said. "One has to think of the differentiation as happening in Anatolia. Then, if one counts back to how long it would take for these dialects to become separate, one has to conclude that the earliest Indo-Europeans must have appeared on the scene by 2300 B.C."

Thus it is possible that Indo-European speakers lived in eastern Anatolia at a time when the people of this area were fashioning impressive artifacts from gold, silver, bronze, lead, and the alloy of gold and silver known as electrum. Such objects, including exquisite filigree gold diadems, bracelets, chalices, daggers, sun disks, and bull and stag figurines, were discovered in 13 "royal" tombs at a site called Alacahöyük less than twenty miles north of Hattusa. Most of what remains of Alacahöyük today — its sphinx-guarded gateway, the foundations of its palace and temple — dates from the Hittite Empire. But Alacahöyük had been inhabited at least since the middle of the third millennium B.C., and the objects from the tombs relate to the earlier period.

The tombs themselves resembled the mound graves, or *kurgans,* of an Indo-European people who migrated from somewhere north of the Caspian and Aral Seas westward into Europe during the third millennium. The possibility exists that they also moved into eastern Anatolia through the Caucasus. Kurgans excavated in the Caucasus and elsewhere were furnished with rich mortuary offerings, including bronze objects resembling those from Alacahöyük. But in discussing the possible ties implied, Dr. Güterbock acknowledges the uncertainty that characterizes so much of Hittite lore: "Now, of course, this is just a theory. It may be right and it may be wrong."

Whenever and however they got to Anatolia, the Hittites appear to have found there a flourishing Bronze Age culture—that of the Hattic people as influenced by the eastern culture of Assyrian merchants who lived in enclaves among them at such places as Kültepe, north of the modern city of Kayseri, and even in old Hattus. The Hittites adopted much of the Hattic culture as their own, including religion and myth, technology, and some of the vocabulary. Scholars continue to search for original Hittite contributions that can be clearly labeled as Indo-European—contributions that go beyond their military and organizational skills, their language, their historical records, and their versions of myths and epics. Though, on the whole, the Hittites seem to have adopted more than they contributed, the matter must be left to further study.

One last great question remains: Where did the Hittites go? Their empire collapsed only two generations after Hattusili III concluded the Egyptian peace treaty, and Hattusa was razed about 1200 B.C. This sudden end has been largely attributed to invasions by "Sea Peoples"—seafarers from the western Mediterranean and points in between. But, as Dr. Neve told me at Hattusa, "we have found not a trace of them."

Some of the Hittites are thought to have dispersed to the south and southeast, where they survived in small, independent city-states. These neo-Hittites, as they are known, abandoned cuneiform writing and used hieroglyphs for the Luwian language exclusively. At such places as Carchemish and Karatepe, they left magnificent reliefs carved in blocks of stone and done in the Hittite style, while showing, with the passage of time, increasingly strong eastern influences. But by the late eighth century B.C., the Assyrians had gained control over the area, and even the neo-Hittites vanished from the Near Eastern scene.

Turkish workmen clear a portion of the outer fortifications of Hattusa. Excavations under the supervision of the German Archaeological Institute have yielded a wealth of information and countless relics, including thousands of inscribed tablets. At right, reassembled jars and basins fill a laboratory workroom at the site.

In haze-filtered sunlight the fertile, wheat-growing Anatolian Plateau rolls northward from the heights of Hattusa's upper city. Atop a stony prominence stand the ruins of the Yenicekale, or "New Castle," a small, isolated structure within the walls of the Hittite capital. The farm town of Boğazkale lies at left, where stately poplars thrust above other trees. Opposite, the rock of Nişantepe bears a hieroglyphic inscription by Suppiluliuma II, last known Hittite king.

PAGES 242-243: *Spring's greening touch tints Hattusa's rocky landscape as Hittite charioteers race outside the city walls. The king watches from his own chariot amid festively dressed courtiers. The annual celebration of spring, most important event in the Hittite calendar, included solemn religious ceremonies as well as merrymaking—and lasted 38 days.*

PAINTING BY DAVID BLOSSOM

Restored foundations of Alacahöyük outline locations of Hittite dwellings (foreground) and a palace complex (background). "Royal" tombs from an even earlier age—the reconstructed chambers at center— yielded a vast hoard of gold and silver artifacts, including the silver-inlaid bronze stag at right. A pair of stone sphinxes from the Hittite period, one of them shown below, flank the gateway to the site. A double-headed eagle appears on the side of the block. Other reliefs nearby depict scenes of worship, lion and stag hunting, and a merry procession with musicians, a sword-swallower, and acrobats.

RIGHT: HIRMER FOTOARCHIV, MUNICH

STAG SHOWN APPROXIMATELY ½ ACTUAL SIZE

Heavy with wool, a flock of unshorn sheep rambles past a spring-fed pond in central Anatolia. A Hittite monument, probably dating from about 1250 B.C., raises carved monoliths capped by a winged sun disk and two lesser suns. Ten demons support the three winged disks; under the lesser suns stand the eroded forms of two deities. As people of the soil, the Hittites had an acute awareness of the importance of water and considered springs sacred. This shrine at Eflatun Pinar, near Beyşehir, combines elements of the farmer's perennial preoccupations: water, earth, and the crop-nurturing sun.

By Cynthia Russ Ramsay
Photographed by David Hiser

LAND OF

THE SINHALESE KINGS

Smoldering incense sticks perfume the darkness. From time to time a murmured chanting ripples across the temple courtyard, where hundreds of tiny coconut-oil lamps twinkle on the stone pavement. In the flickering yellow light, a woman hangs a garland of small prayer flags from a tree festooned with these votive offerings of the faithful.

It is the evening hour of worship, when the pilgrims gather in the sacred precincts. Some arrive in a procession with hands folded in reverence; others bring offerings of lotus flowers. They come from all parts of this tropical island, just off the southern tip of India and only about 500 miles north of the Equator. They come from thatched huts at the edge of rice fields, from rubber and tea plantations, from the cool, verdant mountains of the interior and the lush, palm-shaded coast, and from the crowded streets of Colombo, the port-metropolis and capital of Sri Lanka, a nation slightly larger than West Virginia.

They come to ancient Anuradhapura, a city of crumbling monuments and resurrected Buddhist shrines, of elegant sculpture and stone pillars, some standing, some fallen to the ground. Their Buddhist faith brings them here, for by honoring the images of the Buddha and visiting the age-old shrines, the pilgrims earn merit for their future lives.

I have come on another quest. I am visiting Anuradhapura and will explore the ruins of the long-abandoned cities of Polonnaruwa and Sigiriya to recapture Sri Lanka's remarkable past—that lost time when monarchs and monks, artists and engineers, carpenters and masons led a population of millions in forging a civilization in the northern half of the island that rivaled any in the ancient world.

In the 1,500 years of its greatness—from the 3rd century B.C. to the 13th century A.D.—the Sinhalese Kingdom grew rich on agriculture and trade. Vast fertile fields irrigated with water from man-made reservoirs yielded three bountiful rice harvests a year, and on land greened only by rain farmers grew cotton and sugarcane and raised thriving herds of cattle.

Testimony in stone of past grandeur, foundation pillars of the Brazen Palace provide a serene retreat for a Buddhist monk at Anuradhapura. The 1,600 granite posts recall a splendid, nine-story wooden monastery, said to have contained a thousand rooms. Copper plates covering the roof gave it the name "brazen." Constructed in the 2nd century B.C. by King Dutthagamani, rebuilt many times, the structure finally fell into ruin in the 12th century A.D.

PAGES 248-249: *Caressed by soft morning light, children stroll to school in Anuradhapura. Their path borders the Basawak Kulama, oldest remaining reservoir of the ancient Sinhalese water system.*

Persian, Arab, and Malay fleets crowded island ports to carry pearls, rubies, sapphires, ivory, tortoise shells, and fine muslin cloth to the empires of Rome, India, and China. The Sinhalese kings held court in opulent palaces and delighted in elaborate gardens with pavilions, bathing pools, and fountains. They constructed hospitals and bridges; they paved roads and dammed rivers, and built huge reservoirs as part of an ingenious and complex irrigation system that provided life-giving waters to rice fields over hundreds of square miles.

The wealth and skills of the ancients not only served the needs of the state and the pleasure of royalty but also exalted and embellished the Buddhist religion. Massive domed shrines, some larger than most of the pyramids of Egypt, were built to house sacred relics. Multistoried monasteries, many with pillared sermon halls, accommodated communities of monks that numbered in the thousands. Sculpture graced temples, and statues of the Buddha gave eloquent expression to the population's faith.

But repeated invasions from south India and frequent and prolonged outbreaks of internal strife—palace intrigue and provincial rebellions—eventually depleted the energy and resources of the beleaguered kingdom. Anuradhapura was sacked again and again, and for more than two centuries, beginning in 781, the Sinhalese intermittently used Polonnaruwa, sixty miles to the southeast, as an alternate capital. By 993, when an Indian army stormed ashore and battled its way to Polonnaruwa, both cities had been destroyed.

Then, during a brief but brilliant renaissance that lasted little more than a hundred years, the Sinhalese used their remarkable talents to rebuild Polonnaruwa and create a city of grace and splendor.

In 1215 a major Indian attack dealt the Sinhalese civilization a devastating blow, and thereafter its princes retreated to ever more isolated corners of the land, where they preserved a culture that was a dim, debilitated reflection of the past. In once great cities, deer and elephants roamed the wide thoroughfares. Trees and shrubs rooted and spread in moldering buildings laid waste by war. Rice fields shriveled as irrigation canals dried up and water in neglected reservoirs drained away. Stagnant pools became breeding grounds for mosquitoes that brought the scourge of malaria to the declining realm.

Nineteenth-century photographs show the sacred Ruwanveli Dagoba, one of the giant domed shrines, reduced to a heap of rubble overgrown with vegetation. Looking at the pictures, I sense the desolation of the deserted, decaying place.

But a far different sight greets me as I arrive in Anuradhapura on a sultry February day. From a distance I can see the dome of the restored Ruwanveli Dagoba rising above the horizon of trees, its rock-crystal pinnacle sharp against a Wedgwood-blue sky. I begin my exploration of the city by watching the vivid parade of pilgrims flowing past its base—sari-clad women walking with their special ambling grace, men in shirts and trousers or ankle-length sarongs, pleated and tied with a belt at the waist. A smile shines from every face. Here and there knots of tourists pause to aim their cameras at the frieze of elephants along the dagoba's outer wall and at the flower-strewn altars on its platform base.

"Most of the early dagobas, or stupas, were built of solid brick and coated with a white lime plaster," explains M. H. Sirisoma, assistant commissioner of the government's Department of Archaeology. "Deep inside at the platform level, there is a chamber—a holy-of-holies—that contains either a relic or a sacred symbol of the Buddha. The Thuparama, oldest dagoba in Sri Lanka, was built in the third century B.C. to enshrine a collar-bone relic of the Buddha. And we believe the Ruwanveli once held a golden image of the Buddha and a silver bo tree about 27 feet tall."

The round, spired stupa form was brought to the island from India, land of the Buddha's birth, when Mahinda, missionary son of the Emperor Asoka, came to Sri Lanka about 250 B.C. and converted King Devanampiya Tissa and his court. The event inspired a great flowering of religious architecture, for every stupa, temple, or monastery was more than a testament of faith. It was a good deed that would bring rewards to the monarch and all the workmen in their next incarnations.

Scholars trace the origin of the stupa form to prehistoric burial mounds. In time the immense dome came to represent the vault of heaven, and the structure as a whole symbolized the earth and the cosmos. But there are those who accept another explanation for its dome and triple-tiered base:

"A disciple asked the Buddha, 'What shall we worship after you are gone?'

"The Buddha folded his monk's robe into three layers, placed his inverted begging bowl on top, and replied, 'My teaching alone shall be your teaching. But this is all I have; you can worship that if you must.'"

Five of these monumental relic-tombs dominate Anuradhapura's beguiling landscape of coconut palms and luxuriant, dark green shade trees. To reach the Abhayagiri Dagoba we return to the car that has brought us from Colombo. We stroll or drive from one site to another depending on the distance, for Anuradhapura is one of the largest archaeological sites in the world, sprawling over an area of 25 square miles.

Although vegetation still smothers the Abhayagiri Dagoba, the Department of Archaeology has begun freeing the dome a small section at a time and methodically resetting its bricks layer by layer. It is a considerable undertaking, for according to one calcu-

lation the mound has enough bricks to build a wall one foot thick and ten feet high from London to Edinburgh. "We can't just apply a chemical to kill the plants at once. The whole structure would crumble into a landslide of bricks. The web of roots is now actually holding the bricks in place," says Mr. Sirisoma.

Like their colleagues elsewhere, Sri Lankan archaeologists are committed to a policy of conserving the ruins rather than renovating them. But to Buddhists many of these monuments are much more than relics of the past. They are cherished, living shrines. "So sometimes we in the Department of Archaeology must bow to the demands of the devout who want to bring new sparkle to these worn monuments, even if the results are not historically authentic," Mr. Sirisoma tells me as he leads the way to the most revered place in all Anuradhapura—the Sacred Bo Tree.

Buddhists in the millions have meditated before the tree planted in this spot more than 2,200 years ago. It is said to have come from India, from a branch of the very tree under which the Buddha sat when he attained enlightenment. Flower stalls line the walkway to the compound where the tree stands. Only lotus buds are for sale. I buy one and am informed that the lotus is not a proper offering until it can emit its sweet fragrance to the world. So I open the petals one by one, joining the religious pageant all around me.

A gentle reminder from Mr. Sirisoma tells me that in every sacred area, shoes are removed and left at the gate. I walk barefoot across the courtyard, past the image house, or temple, where a modern statue of the Buddha reclines glossy with bright enamel, a soft, secret half-smile on its face. I stop at the enclosure around the base of the Bo Tree. Now, as in ages past, people place their offerings of flowers on a simple stone altar and with bowed heads repeat verses old in Caesar's time. The words, recited in Pali, the ancient language of the Buddhist scriptures, are whispered to me in English by my learned companion: "With these beautiful flowers, emblems of beauty and purity, I worship Thee, Lord Buddha. As these blossoms will fade and die, in the same manner I too will fade and wither away." But encircled by a wall and a golden rail, its single, gnarled branch supported by five iron props, the Bo Tree endures.

It is a more successful survivor than the fabled Brazen Palace, whose nine stories have succumbed to fire, vandalism, and time. Like most buildings in Anuradhapura, the Brazen Palace was built mainly of wood and was destroyed and rebuilt many times. Now all that remains of the structure, which once housed hundreds of monks and provided them with a great assembly hall, is row upon row of square-cut granite pillars—a forest of 1,600 columns, gray, gaunt, and disquieting, brooding over a vanished world.

Monks wrote of "that renowned palace" with poetry, enthusiasm, and perhaps a little exaggeration in the *Mahavamsa*, the chronicle of early Sinhalese kings. Inscribed on dried leaves of the talipot palm in the fifth century A.D., the epic records traditional descriptions of the Brazen Palace but was composed several centuries after the building had been completed— leaving to scholars the task of sifting fact from legend and fantasy.

". . . nine stories, and in each story a hundred window-chambers . . . all overlaid with silver . . . a gem pavilion set up in the middle . . . adorned with pillars consisting of precious stones, on which were figures of lions, tigers, and . . . shapes of goddesses. . . .

"Within . . . stood a shining beauteous throne of ivory with a seat of mountain-crystal, and in the ivory back . . . a sun in gold, a moon in silver, and stars in pearls, and lotus blossoms made of various gems. . . .

"Costly beds and chairs, according to rank, and carpets and coverlets of great price. . . . the palace gleamed in its magnificence like the hall in heaven. . . . [It] was covered over with plates of copper, and thence came its name 'Brazen Palace.'"

Over the years schisms developed and split the monks into separate orders. In time, a total of four major monastic communities received such royal patronage, acquired so much land, and amassed such wealth and power that ancient Anuradhapura was the site of 3,000 to 4,000 monastic buildings.

The small sounds of birds drift through the trees as I pick my way through the ruins known today as the Western Monasteries. Since 1890, when the island's first office of archaeology was established, workers have dug deep into the rich dark soil to expose platforms, columns, and stairways—the stone remains of buildings that served the monks' simple needs.

Where I wander, monks in robes of saffron yellow once meditated in small, solitary cells; they listened to sermons, discussed the scriptures, and confessed their offenses in the large public halls. Now cattle graze beside these stone edges of antiquity. A boy from the village just beyond sits on a step, studying me while sucking the pulp from a (Continued on page 258)

"Gem of the Summer Sea," a 19th-century visitor called the tropical island known to the West then as Ceylon and now as Sri Lanka. From about the 3rd century B.C. until the 13th century A.D., an extraordinary civilization flourished here. Closely identified with the Buddhist faith, Anuradhapura, the first capital, included more than 3,000 monastic structures. In the 11th century the Sinhalese rulers moved to Polonnaruwa, where both art and architecture reached a peak before the kingdom's rapid dissolution.

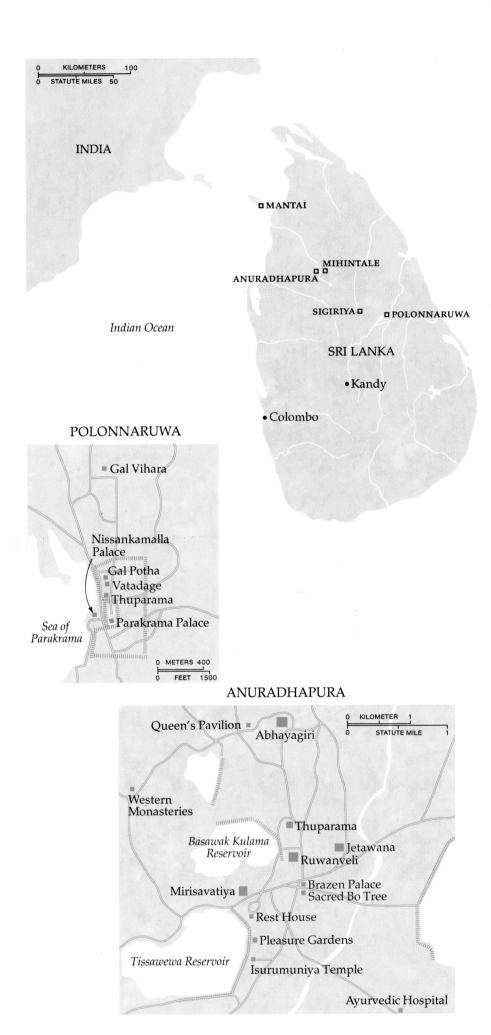

253

Glowing lamps illuminate paths of pilgrims making their way to shrines at Mihintale, the "very cradle of Buddhism in Ceylon." Seven miles from Anuradhapura, the cluster of sanctuaries marks the place where in the third century B.C. Mahinda, missionary son of the Indian emperor Asoka, confronted the Sinhalese king Devanampiya Tissa.

Tradition relates that the king and his hunting party—an incredible entourage of 40,000—pursued a stag to the thicket-covered mountain, where they encountered Mahinda. At center, a small dagoba called Ambastala, meaning "mango tree," commemorates the spot where Mahinda tested the depth of the king's intellect with a subtle riddle about mangoes. Satisfied, he then converted Devanampiya Tissa to the new religion. Relics of the missionary lie protected within Ambastala. The large dagoba in the background enshrines a hair-relic of the Buddha.

Buddhism permeates Sri Lankan society. Hands pressed together in reverence, two monks bow their heads before the Sacred Bo Tree at Anuradhapura. Carved elephants keep watch; stout poles support the single gnarled branch of the tree, grown from a cutting from the tree in India where the Buddha attained enlightenment. A jubilant procession, the chroniclers report, accompanied the precious twig on its journey in 247 B.C. across the island to its present site. A "beautiful car" bore it along a "road sprinkled with white sand, bestrewn with various flowers . . . and festoons of blossoms." Sri Lankans today heed any decline of the 2,000-year-old tree as a portent of disaster. Any new shoot—no matter how small—bodes good fortune. At left, a monk meditates in a cave at Mihintale, where Buddhism first came to Sri Lanka. He will spend three months living here, away from his monastery, to renew his concentration on the goal of achieving nirvana or ultimate bliss.

*Threshold to wisdom, a finely carved "moonstone"
serves as the first step to the Queen's Pavilion temple
at Anuradhapura. Buddhism inspired much of the
artistry of ancient Sri Lanka to symbolism beyond
mere decoration. Some scholars find a message about
the nature of human existence in the stone semicircles
usually found at shrine entrances: The flames in the
outer rim of the eighth-century carving signify the
passions that envelop mankind. A parade of animals,
in this interpretation, stands for the never-ending
perils of life: birth, disease, old age, and death.
Geese, holding lotus blossoms in their bills, allude
to awakening discernment. And the central lotus
motif stands for the attainment of understanding.*

half-peeled orange. A man strolls by, cigar in mouth
and soap dish in hand, on his way to take a bath in the
canal nearby.

So much of ancient Anuradhapura has disappeared, the timbers of its buildings devoured by fire or
the elements, the bricks reduced to dust, and so much
remains still to be excavated, that the layout of the city
is not immediately apparent. An enlightening dis-
course days before by Roland Silva, an urbane architect and deputy commissioner of archaeology, helps
me fit what I have seen into an overall plan.

"A wall enclosed the inner city, where the monarch and members of his court resided, and weavers,
potters, jewelers, and other craftsmen sold their
wares. Outside the walls, at a prescribed distance of no
less than 500 bow-lengths from the four city gates,
stood the various monasteries, each with its dagoba,
temple, and monastic buildings. Beyond this inner
ring lay a middle circle of reservoirs and village fields
and houses, then an outer ring consisting of smaller
forest monasteries."

Deciding to wait a day to see the reservoirs, I retire
to the Tissawewa Rest House, a rambling wooden
structure left over from the British colonial past. The
wide verandas and lush, landscaped garden, the large
ceiling fans and beds draped in mosquito netting offer
nostalgic atmosphere as well as comfort.

Next morning, I set out for the Tissawewa Reservoir. As the amber light of sunrise spreads across the
sky, I walk past a village that has grown up around the
restored tank. Tendrils of smoke from cooking fires
drift above the mellow bronze of rice ready for harvest.
A bullock cart lumbers by. Well-scrubbed children in
starched uniforms turn to smile at me on their way to
school. A little girl stands in a doorway while her
mother plaits her hair into two plump braids.

Suddenly I am not alone. Santha, who is 12 years
old, runs to catch up with me and holds out a small
pink rose. He has sparkling eyes, a mischievous grin,
and a good command of English. He turns my excur-
sion into a delightful ramble across the countryside.

Although he has stopped going to school because
his "shirt is no good," Santha has a fund of knowledge
which he imparts with gallantry and charm. He finds a
mimosa whose tiny leaves fold up at our touch. He
discovers a gecko, or tropical lizard, flattened against
the bark of a tree. He splits the purple pod that hangs
from a kapok tree to show me the silky cotton inside.

We detour to the Isurumuniya Temple, one of the
many temples chiseled into solid rock. Concealed by
jungle for hundreds of years, it was rediscovered in the
19th century. Now its restored, freshly painted white
portico stands prettily beside a square pool in a setting
of sculpture and trees.

Stone elephants gambol along the lower face of
the outcrop where it rises from the glossy surface of the

ritual pool. The charm and vitality of the bas-relief express the joy of frolicking in the water. Nearby, another masterpiece known as "The Lovers" conveys a gentler, tender mood.

Like the sudden streak of a shooting star, a bird dives down to the pool in a flash of turquoise and pauses for a few seconds on the petals of a water lily to reward us with its beauty. We wait awhile for the kingfisher to return, and then ascend the steps cut into the rock. They lead us over the top of the temple, and we find ourselves just below the embankment of the Tissawewa Reservoir.

Left to myself, I would fail to appreciate fully the engineering achievement of the ancient irrigation system. I have had the good fortune, however, to meet Professor R. A. L. H. Gunawardana, a youngish scholar who has delved diligently into his country's past. He received me in his home on the campus of Peredeniya University, just outside the hill town of Kandy. In a cultured British accent he described the technology necessary to build dams that impounded water over areas as large as 6,400 acres with sections of embankment as long as seven miles.

"Not only did the engineers develop the capacity to move vast amounts of earth, but they also solved the problems of releasing great volumes of water at a manageable flow. Certain embankments retained water to depths of 35 or 40 feet. Water released from reservoirs of such depth exerts tremendous pressure which, if not controlled, would destroy embankments as it surged through the culverts.

"But by the second century A.D. the engineers had devised a workable system. Sluices were placed at staggered levels in the embankment and valve mechanisms were installed to control the openings, so water was discharged at a tolerable pressure.

"The water was then transported to the fields by a network of canals totaling more than 200 miles. Survey techniques and instruments were so sophisticated and precise that the Sinhalese were able to maintain gradients as slight as an astonishing six inches a mile.

"It was this knowledge and skill that made large-scale irrigation possible throughout the year, giving the kingdom the agricultural surplus to sustain the impetus to grandeur.

"There is evidence," he concluded, "to suggest the ancients knew the earth was round. We have still to discern the full extent of their achievements in astronomy, mathematics, and engineering."

In the field of medicine, there is more information and more continuity. Pandit William Alwis still treats his patients in ways prescribed by medical texts handed down through centuries of Sri Lanka's recorded history.

Intrigued by the remains of an ancient hospital near Anuradhapura and reports of remarkable cures by physicians still practicing the traditional Ayurvedic medicine, I am determined to secure an interview with the highly respected Pandit Alwis.

I step out of the glare and cacophony of one of Colombo's main streets into the calm of his spacious house. My first question is prompted by the stone bath, cut to the shape of a human body, that I have seen in the ruins of the hospital.

"It was filled with herbal oils," Pandit Alwis explains. "Patients suffering from rheumatism and victims of snakebite were submerged in such baths for massage treatments that would last for hours.

"We still use massage extensively—even for circulatory problems. With massage, circulation becomes rapid and easy, and then the blood can carry away the fatty particles accumulated in the veins and arteries.

"Our medicines are herbal preparations, and they are bringing us great success in dealing with arthritis.

"Though the ancient texts tell us the King Buddhadasa practiced surgery as far back as the fourth century, I send my patients to doctors of western medicine for operations and treatment of malaria," he readily concedes.

But neither achievements in science nor accomplishments in art convey much of what life is like in the villages where the majority of Sri Lankans have always lived. On the way to Polonnaruwa, at the edge of the ancient city, we drive across the embankment of the Parakrama Samudra, or Sea of Parakrama, a reservoir attributed to the 12th-century monarch Parakrama Bahu the Great, whose many building projects were part of an ambitious plan to make his capital as magnificent as Anuradhapura itself. Near the shore, black, barren trees stand half-submerged, leafless specters left over from a recent past when vegetation clogged the reservoir.

Ainnsley Sirisena, driver, translator, and my ambassador-at-large, turns off the main road and heads toward Kalahagala, a village whose rice fields receive water from the Parakrama Samudra. There, in ways little changed from those of their forefathers, farmers still drive water buffalo to plow the mudlands; they still stand ankle-deep in water to plant the rice seedlings by hand; and they still toil, backs bent low, in the timeless rites of harvest.

We pull up beside a rice mill (there *are* some changes) and walk single file on a narrow path to the village. Barefoot children swarm around me. Naturally polite like their parents, they form a persistent but surprisingly sedate entourage.

The trees in Uttama Pusumbi Ammavallie's yard bring forth oranges, papayas, passion fruit, bananas, mangoes, tamarinds, jackfruit, and coconuts in bountiful anarchy. Uttama, a slender, unmatronly-looking

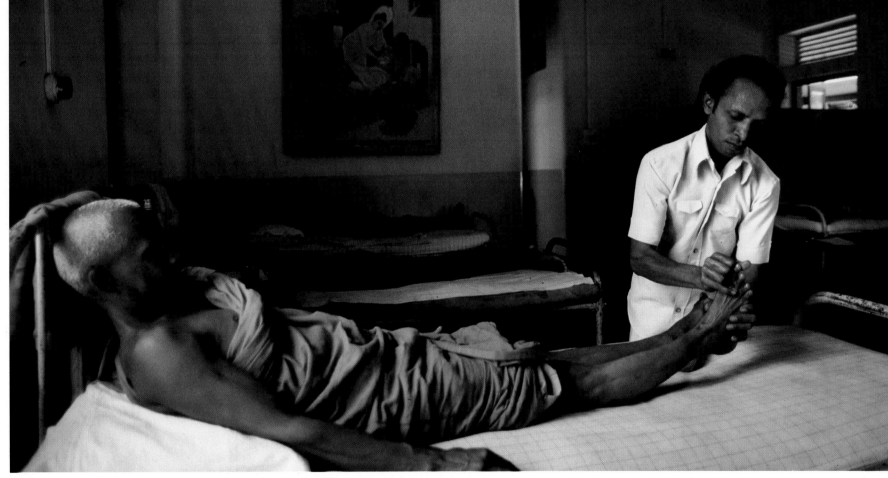

*H*ealing hands ease the aches of an ailing monk at the Ayurvedic Hospital at Anuradhapura, echoing a scene on the wall of the Buddha tending an ill holy man. The Ayurveda, or "science of long and healthy life," makes use of ancient oil and herbal remedies and massage techniques. A pharmacy worker at the 120-bed hospital prepares medicinal oils in a copper caldron. At top, mixtures of leaves, thorns, tree heart, and castor beans, with prescriptions tucked in, await delivery to patients. Myth links the medical system to the Hindu god Brahma himself, and written references to it in India occur as early as 1000 B.C. Excavations have revealed extensive hospital centers in ancient Sri Lanka.

mother of ten children, steps out of her house and greets me with formal courtesy. Refreshments are offered. Ainnsley opts for *bulat vita,* a betel leaf dusted with lime powder and wrapped around an astringent betel nut and bits of cardamom and cloves. It is the popular chew that produces the blood-red spittle staining the streets of all south Asia. I accept a coconut, fresh from a tree and sliced at the top. As I tilt my head back to pour the clear, slightly saline liquid into my mouth, it drips undaintily down my chin.

Uttama knows happiness. She and her people are happy if the rains come on time, if their crops are good, and if they have enough to eat. And they are happy when they go to the temple. Ainnsley elaborates: "There is no life for the villagers without the temple. On the first day of sowing, they go to the temple, and after harvest, they take a quota of grain to the temple. When someone falls sick, when husband and wife quarrel, they go to the temple."

This allegiance to the temple and its monks has been traced to ancient times by the scholar Walpola Rahula. In his *History of Buddhism in Ceylon,* he wrote: "... the monk was the most trusted teacher and guide and friend of the people. He intervened at all critical moments and settled their disputes—even in state affairs. In all matters great and small, people went to him for advice, guidance, and consolation."

And on the Poya Days, the holy days of the full moon, even the ordinary laymen will observe some of the precepts monks vow to obey throughout their lives. Each month, when temple bells and temple drums summon the congregation, families gather in the temple—all simply clad in freshly laundered white. On that day the devout do not eat after the noon hour; they do not wear ornaments, use cosmetics, distract themselves with singing, music, or dance, or rest on cushioned, comfortable beds or seats.

"The Poya Days give every Buddhist who observes the precepts the opportunity once a month to experience the discipline of the ascetic life," said Piyadassi Thera, a monk whose wisdom, learning, and piety have made him a spokesman for Sri Lanka's Theravada branch of Buddhism around the world. To learn about the doctrines of Buddhism, I had called upon him in Colombo in the courtyard of his temple, Vajirarama, where he received the reverent bows of his disciples by blessing them with a slight nod.

"The Buddha perceived that sorrow and suffering stem from the craving for things animate and inanimate, for life's fleeting and illusory pleasures. At his enlightenment the Buddha found a way to overcome these desires. The Noble Eight-fold Path is the key: right view, right thought, right speech, right action, right livelihood, right effort, right mindfulness, right

Honored emblem of royalty and patient beast of burden, the elephant has contributed its dignity and strength to Sri Lanka through the centuries. Wielding tusks and trunks (opposite), elephants move huge logs and boulders in the jungles of ancient Sri Lanka to clear the way for a reservoir. Cut stones await placement in a sluice wall. The brute strength of the gentle creatures joined with the remarkable engineering skills of the ancient Sinhalese to create the irrigation network that formed the very foundation of their civilization. Today a huge "tusker" dwarfs his mahout, or keeper, as he lumbers along a road near Colombo on the way to work.

Irrigated rice fields shimmer a lush green near Polonnaruwa. Even neglected and fallen into ruin, remnants of the ancient Sinhalese irrigation system represented for 19th-century historian Sir Emerson Tennent "the proudest monuments . . . of the former greatness of the country." The Sinhalese created enormous reservoirs that enabled them to produce plentiful food during prolonged dry periods. The key to their success lay in an ingenious cistern-sluice that allowed the release of water from tanks thirty or forty feet deep without destroying embankments. The sluice at left once handled water flow for the Royal Pleasure Garden at Anuradhapura. Efforts continue to restore old waterways to help increase today's crop yields.

concentration. That is Buddhism in practice. It is a code of behavior, a spiritual self-improvement plan, that mastered step by step will eventually extinguish desire and lead to the bliss of nirvana."

"What is nirvana?" I asked. He repeated my question with no hint of impatience. "Can you explain what quenching one's thirst is like? It is something that must be experienced. In the same way nirvana is not for theorizing; it is for realizing.

"But more than nirvana," he continued, "Buddha showed mankind how to escape the pain of birth, death, and rebirth. And release from that cycle is the ultimate goal of Buddhism."

A combination of gentleness, serenity, and great dignity, the Venerable Piyadassi embodies the virtues extolled by his Buddhist faith. A few days later, when I met with architect-archaeologist Roland Silva a second time, he analyzed Buddhism from another angle. He defined its doctrines as an economic force that enriched the realm: "By upholding the ascetic ideal, Buddhism encourages each person to minimize his wants. Fewer needs leave more spare time. The religion also exhorts its followers to perform good deeds as an investment in their next incarnation, for wealth, beauty, intelligence, and power can be the results of merit accumulated in a previous lifetime.

"With time to spare and such an incentive, the population—from king to humblest villager—volunteered supplies and labor for the construction of religious buildings and monuments. These donations

Massive images of the Buddha, hewn out of the living stone of this hillside in the 12th century, impart to the faithful the greatness of their Master. The 46-foot-long recumbent figure at Gal Vihara in Polonnaruwa represents the Buddha at the instant of achieving nirvana. The standing figure shows the Buddha gazing with compassion on the sorrows of mankind.

were a major source of material and manpower for the benefit of the kingdom and its powerful monasteries."

At Polonnaruwa, masons must have been remarkably busy, for the towering walls of its palaces and temples were made of brick. Much more durable than wooden structures, the buildings of Polonnaruwa evoke the past more readily than the litter of vague fragments and modern restorations scattered across the broad expanse of older Anuradhapura.

The royal quarter with its palace, audience hall,

Mahavamsa, and the blank walls around me become rooms where people lived. There were pillars painted in many colors, beds of gold and ivory, and decorations of plants and flowers. Thick bunches of pearls hung from the four corners of the royal bedchamber, where golden bells and golden lamps provided the monarch with music and light. It is easy to imagine the great building filled with ladies of the court draped in shawls of diaphanous silk, their sleek hair decorated with flowers; servants by the hundred and guards with daggers and swords; dancers, musicians, courtiers, and the king himself, bare to the waist and wearing a crown ablaze with jewels.

The whole city must have trembled with excitement as musicians blowing conch shells announced the royal procession to the audience hall, where the monarch received his ministers and generals. Now sunlight floods the stone skeleton of the hall, and the loudest sound is the schooled voice of a tourist guide drawing attention to the lively carvings of elephants, lions, and gnomes that decorate the three tiers of the building's platform base.

Nissankamalla, the last of Sri Lanka's notable kings, built his own palace and council chamber, with pillars inscribed to show where each minister was to take his place. He presided over meetings of state from a throne set on a huge figure of a lion.

*I*f I had only one hour to spend in Polonnaruwa, I would drive past the palaces and the circular relic houses, past the stone pool in the form of a lotus flower and the Hindu temples which recall the Indian occupation, and I would go to see the four giant figures of the Buddha at the Gal Vihara.

There, unknown sculptors transformed a single granite escarpment into the essence of serenity and spiritual vitality. With that elusive alchemy of skill and inspiration, artists turned stone into the subtle textures of skin, created the soft effect of flesh, and touched the face of the Buddha with compassion.

Time fades away before the vibrant stillness of the reclining Buddha and the gentle, sympathetic air of the standing figure; but the hour must also include a visit to the impressive 12-foot sculpture of a bearded sage or king. Clearly a portrait, believed by some to be Parakrama Bahu himself, the statue conveys the authority and strength of a great personality—someone it would have been fascinating to meet.

Out of the mist of Sri Lanka's past, kings of many shades of character emerge—builders, warriors, patrons of art, practitioners of medicine. Some who were brutal in battle became pious and benevolent in peace. None is more baffling than Kassapa, the fifth-century monarch who abandoned Anuradhapura and ruled his kingdom from Sigiriya, an immense outcrop of

and park lies just a few hundred yards from a quadrangle of sacred buildings. Enormous walls—11 feet thick and 40 feet high—shade me from the late afternoon sun as I prowl through the shell of Parakrama Bahu's palace. Giant grooves in the brick once held wooden pillars to support beams for a ceiling now open to the sky. Stone steps, which once ascended to upper floors, lead me a short distance to nowhere.

I remember some of the descriptions in the *Chulavamsa*, the chronicle that is a continuation of the earlier

*B*rick by brick, devout Sri Lankans earn religious merit by rebuilding sacred structures at Anuradhapura. Crumbling and overgrown with vegetation, the Abhayagiri Dagoba (below) awaits complete restoration. When enlarged in the fourth century, the shrine soared to a height of 400 feet and equaled in mass the Third Pyramid at Giza. Opposite, work progresses on the Mirisavatiya Dagoba. Bricks salvaged from the old structure for reuse lie in a jumble in the foreground. Workers follow a steel template fixed above the structure to determine the final contour, different from the original. Such changes pit archaeologists who want to preserve and study ancient architectural forms against believers who find improvement in modernization. According to legend, this dagoba acquired its name, which means "chili pod," when King Dutthagamani built it as penance for forgetting once to fulfill a fundamental Buddhist obligation: setting aside for the monks a portion of his meal—in this case a pepper curry.

granite that rises abruptly from placid green fields like a colossal meteorite that has plunged from the sky.

The rock rests in the sun, gathering the heat of the day. By midafternoon, when I begin my ascent, it seems I am inhaling the breath of some unseen beast.

Kassapa, according to the chronicles, murdered his father and usurped his brother's throne. In fear of reprisal, he fled from the capital and sought protection in a citadel stronghold. But the late Dr. Senarat Paranavitana, former commissioner of the Department of Archaeology, argued that Kassapa was vilified by the partisan monks writing the account. Kassapa, he believed, withdrew to Sigiriya not as a fugitive but as an idealist seeking to create a paradise retreat.

Eighteen years later—say the chronicles—when his avenging brother marched on Sigiriya with a new army, Kassapa left the safety of his aerie home, then took his own life during a battle on the plain below. Did he leave his fortress because fear and guilt had sapped his will to live, or because he loved his creation too much to see it marred and destroyed?

Sanctuary or Shangri-La, Sigiriya's fame resides in the frescoes I am climbing to see. Halfway to the top, I wait my turn to step into the natural gallery in the rock formed by an overhanging wall. I am unprepared for the beauty I find. All the praise lavished on these utterly lovely women—celestial nymphs or ladies of the court—fails to convey the glow of color and the charm of the graceful forms.

Only 18 figures of the 500 originals survive. They illustrate no story, expressing instead a sublime vision of sensuous, exquisite femininity.

The sun is low, draining color from the sky by the time I reach the ruins on the summit. Only palace foundations and empty pools and reservoirs remain.

As the landscape and fragments of the past dissolve in the dusk, I descend from the heights, my journey ended. With the help of scholars and friends, I have traced the outlines of a great civilization. Its legacy of beauty and fervent belief has no end, for they transcend time. That legacy lingers in every lotus petal placed at the Buddha's feet, in every lamp lit at a religious shrine, and in the bright glow of memories that crowd my mind.

Wealth of sculpture lies scattered through the ever-encroaching jungles of Sri Lanka. An eroded guardstone, displaying a prince with a sweeping multiheaded-cobra headdress, rises out of the rank vegetation to warn the impure of spirit away from a now-vanished Buddhist temple near Anuradhapura. The sinuous lines of the statue borrow from the art motifs of Hindu India.

*M*edieval capital of Sri Lanka, Polonnaruwa sprawls across the tree-studded plain. Sacred precincts called the Quadrangle lie in the foreground. The Vatadage, a circular reliquary at far right, once had a domed roof. At lower left stands the still-covered Hindu-style Thuparama. Numerous raids from southern India forced the Sinhalese in the 11th century to move their seat of government to this more easily defended site 60 miles southeast of Anuradhapura. "The hero, to whom all right-minded people were devoted," the Chulavamsa chroniclers judged King Parakrama Bahu the Great, builder of palaces, temples, and irrigation works that brought the new capital to its zenith in the mid-12th century. His successor, Nissankamalla, claimed for himself much credit for Polonnaruwa's magnificence. A 26-foot-long monolith—the Gal Potha or Stone Book, left and above—hauled from Anuradhapura and inscribed in archaic Sinhalese, boasts of his exploits.

Paying homage, pilgrims pause before a figure of the Buddha in the Vatadage at Polonnaruwa. After flourishing for several generations, the city followed Anuradhapura into oblivion. Some historians attribute the mysterious collapse of the ancient Sri Lankan kingdom to repeated invasions from India, coupled with neglect of the irrigation system. By the late 13th century the jungle had intruded, and it concealed the abandoned city for the next 500 years. Travelers in the 1820s glimpsed the ruins, but excavation did not begin until 1900.

FOLLOWING PAGES: *"Amongst all the ladies of the harem, many hundreds in number, she was by far his best loved . . . skilful in dance and song," writes the chronicler of Queen Rupavati, wife of King Parakrama Bahu the Great. Gliding and twisting into a stylized S-curve, she performs for the king in the dance pavilion of 12th-century Polonnaruwa. The artist relied on detailed descriptions in the* Chulavamsa *to re-create the long-vanished building. The king takes his ease under a pearl-fringed umbrella, symbol of royal authority. On his breast gleams a ruby so splendid that Marco Polo termed it "the grandest ruby that ever was seen."*

Coward's retreat or abode for a god-king? An engineering marvel of palaces, pleasure gardens, and temples once crowned the 600-foot-high outcropping of Sigiriya. Opposite, visitors pass through the remains of the awesome Lion Gate, located a third of the way to the top. Scholars puzzle over what motivated King Kassapa I to haul massive amounts of materials up a virtually unscalable rock to create the elaborate three-acre complex. Some conclude from the chronicles that the king—who had killed his father and usurped his brother's throne—"betook himself through fear" to the stronghold. Others believe that Kassapa, attempting to deify himself, patterned the citadel after an Indian concept of a heavenly city. Obviously in no hurry, the sovereign took years to build a dwelling worthy of a god, and he barely fortified it. Challenged by his brother 18 years later, in the year 495, Kassapa met him and his army on the plain below; but in the ensuing confusion the king, isolated, died by his own hand.

Celestial nymphs rise out of billowy clouds to continue King Kassapa's heavenly theme at Sigiriya. From what once numbered in the hundreds, 18 fresco figures survive in a sheltered alcove in the western face of the great granite monolith. Using rich earth colors of red, yellow, and green, the artists painted over layers of lime and plaster. Perhaps representing cloud damsels and lightning princesses called apsaras, or perhaps merely bejeweled noblewomen of the court, the lively paintings have enchanted visitors through the centuries. More than 700 graffiti, scratched on adjacent walls, record reactions to the "winsome, deer-eyed ones." For one ninth-century visitor after seeing the "resplendent ladies . . . heaven appears . . . as not good." For another, thereafter "death does not perturb."

$\mathcal{F}$*ragile blossoms and glowing incense sticks mix their fragrances during the Poson Festival at Anuradhapura. Clad in traditional white, the devout move among the sacred places of the ancient capital, some to offer flowers with words of veneration: "As these flowers dry up . . . so will my body . . . turn to dust." Pilgrims depart after paying homage at the Ruwanveli Dagoba (opposite), grandest of all the shrines. The holiday, observed each June at the full moon, commemorates the coming of Buddhism to Sri Lanka more than 22 centuries ago.*

*F*estival atmosphere prevails as the gathering crowd prepares to camp under shade trees in the center of Anuradhapura. Hundreds of thousands travel from throughout the island for the three-day Poson. Many come on foot, aided by offers of food and shelter along the way. In the hope of earning merit for the next life, volunteers (below) prepare huge pots of food to be offered free to all.

FOLLOWING PAGES: *Crowning achievement of a king, Ruwanveli Dagoba gleams in the Poson full moon. King Dutthagamani built the original shrine for relics of the Buddha. The chronicles record that the king directed that he be borne around the unfinished structure just before he died. Handsomely renovated in the 19th century, the shrine serves as a major focal point for pilgrimages. The terracotta elephants in the surrounding wall symbolize protection for the relics within.*

Notes on Contributors

Now a resident of the United States, Mehmet Biber was born in a region of Bulgaria that was formerly part of the Ottoman Empire. His knowledge of Turkish was invaluable in carrying out an assignment that took him into the heart of Anatolia. Biber has won Turkish, U. S., and international awards for his photography.

Ira Block's most recent previous assignment for the National Geographic Society was to traverse the United States making a pictorial record to illustrate the Special Publication *Back Roads America*. He also contributed to the popular book *Nature's Healing Arts*. A native of New York, Block attended the University of Wisconsin. His avocations include running and amateur archaeology.

Painter David Blossom is the son and the father of other successful illustrators. Trained at the Yale School of Fine Arts and the Art Students League, he has had a prolific career in book and magazine illustration, including advertising, and was formerly an art director for the J. Walter Thompson agency. He has lived in Weston, Connecticut, since he was 8 years old.

The widely traveled Victor R. Boswell, Jr., has covered assignments on five continents. For *Splendors of the Past* alone he visited England, France, East and West Germany, Italy, and Turkey, as well as four American states. A specialist in still-life photography, Boswell is credited with solving many difficult technical problems posed by conditions of interior lighting and museum display.

Versatile curator of Chicago's famed Oriental Institute Museum, John Carswell brings to his position the skills and experience of archaeologist, artist, and writer. Born in England, he lived in the Middle East for more than twenty years before settling his family in Chicago in 1977. He recently produced, as editor and co-author, the comprehensive volume *Islamic Bindings & Bookmaking*.

Free-lance writer Louis de la Haba has been a frequent contributor to National Geographic Special Publications and to the Society's magazine, where he worked from 1963 to 1974. He is a graduate of Amherst College and earned an M.A. in anthropology from the George Washington University. He is a native of San Juan, Puerto Rico, and has lived in Virginia since 1961.

Former newspaperman Seymour L. Fishbein has been a writer-editor of National Geographic Society books since 1962, and developed an interest in ancient history as associate editor of *Greece and Rome*, *Great Religions of the World*, and *Everyday Life in Bible Times*. A naval aviator during World War II and the Korean War, he now pilots a canoe in summer and skis in the winter.

A resident of Aspen, Colorado, since 1964, David Hiser has been a regular participant in National Geographic Society publishing projects for more than a dozen years, contributing to numerous books—most recently *Trails West*—and 15 magazine articles. An Ohio native, he graduated from the University of Washington and has become a confirmed westerner and mountaineer.

Midwesterner Thomas O'Neill was born in Ohio, grew up in Illinois, and graduated from Beloit College in Wisconsin. A member of the Geographic staff since 1976, he has previously contributed to the Special Publications *Into the Wilderness* and *America's Majestic Canyons* and was the author of *Back Roads America*.

This is the ninth of the National Geographic Special Publications to which Cynthia Russ Ramsay has contributed chapters. A graduate of Hunter College with a major in archaeology, she also participated in a program of South Asian Studies at the University of Pennsylvania. She has since lived in both India and Iran, and has traveled extensively in the Middle East.

For eight years a United States Marine, for nine years a staff artist for the National Geographic Society, Lloyd K. Townsend is now a free-lance illustrator specializing in historical, archaeological, and technical subjects. The Detroit native lives with his wife and children in a century-old Victorian house that they are restoring in Maytown, Pennsylvania.

Born in San Francisco, Michael S. Yamashita has lived in Japan, Thailand, and Singapore as well as in the United States. From his home in New Jersey, he continues to work all over the world. A veteran of several major articles for National Geographic magazine, he photographed the Kingdom of Kush chapter for this volume as his first assignment for the Special Publications Division.

Acknowledgments

The Special Publications Division is grateful to the individuals and organizations named or quoted in the text and to those cited here for their generous cooperation and assistance during the preparation of this book: W. P. S. Anuradha, William Gardner Bell, Robert D. Biggs, Michel A. Boutin, Maya Chadda, Miguel Civil, Maude deSchauensee, Richard S. Fiske, Martine Fivel, McGuire Gibson, Madeleine Giteau, Chester Gorman, Basil Gray, Bernard P. Groslier, the Venerable Henepola Gunaratana, Figen Güray, Süha Güray, Hans G. Güterbock, Donald P. Hansen, William Heimdahl, Alice Jugie, Martine Laurens, Erle Leichty, Mary M. Littauer, Eleanor Mannika, Betty Jo Mayeske, Machteld Mellink, Jennifer Moseley, Walter Rainboth, Joe D. Seger, H. L. Seneviratne, Peter L. Shinnie, Ephraim Stern, Murat Sungar, Raci Temizer, Gus Van Beek, Herbert Weiner, Delande S. Wijeratne,

Bob Zehring, Uza Zevulun; Antiquities Commission, Democratic Republic of the Sudan; Embassy of Sri Lanka; Museum Haaretz, Tel Aviv; Sri Lanka Department of Archaeology.

The artifacts pictured in this volume have been made available by courtesy of the following: Archaeological Museum of Istanbul, 89, 222; Ashmolean Museum, Oxford, 233; British Library, London, 91 lower; Damascus National Museum, 63; Guimet Museum, Paris, 195 right, 198, 206, 216-217; Iraq Museum, Baghdad, 50, 62; Kabul Museum, 29; Louvre Museum, Paris, 99 right, 295; Metropolitan Museum of Art, New York, 64 center left; Museum of Ancient Anatolian Civilizations, Ankara, 245 right, 291; Museum of Fine Arts, Boston, 149 upper; National Archaeological Museum, Naples, 4-5, 120 lower, 123-127, 135 lower, 137, 138-139, 138 center, 141 upper; Norbert Schimmel Collection, 234-235; Oriental Institute, University of Chicago, 34-35, 58 lower, 64 lower left, 70 upper; Rippon Boswell & Co., London, 90; Rockefeller Archaeological Museum, Jerusalem, 75 right; State Collection of Egyptian Art, Munich, 150-151; Sudan National Museum, Khartoum, 159; Trustees of the British Museum, London, 46 left, 48 upper, 49 upper, 53 upper; University Museum, University of Pennsylvania, Philadelphia, 39 upper, 44-45, 46 right, 47, 48 lower, 56 lower, 67 right, 149 center, 149 lower; Peter N. Talkington, 91 upper.

"Like a lamp that dispels darkness . . . dispel my ignorance," a pilgrim murmurs as she ignites tiny cups of coconut oil at the Sacred Bo Tree. The Buddhist tradition remains the unbroken link between the greatness of Sri Lanka's ancient civilization and the present day.

Index

Geometric designs and a circle of sunrays surround an animal figure probably representing a wild ass. Archaeologists believe such devices may have topped ceremonial staffs or royal scepters. Fashioned in bronze more than 4,000 years ago, this artifact came from a rich and sophisticated culture that existed in Asia Minor before the arrival of the people we know as the Hittites.

BAKA GELENBEVI/RAPHO
DEVICE APPROXIMATELY 9 INCHES HIGH

292

Stag flees from a chariot-borne archer in this rubbing of a stone bas-relief. The sculpture echoes Hittite artwork, although carved 300 years after dissolution of the Hittite Empire. Successor city-states emerged in southeastern Anatolia and Syria, and for a time the people—now called neo-Hittites—used Hittite names and hieroglyphs and worshiped Hittite gods.

BAS-RELIEF APPROXIMATELY 13 BY 29 INCHES

Additional Reading

The reader may want to check the *National Geographic* Index for related articles and to refer to the following books: AN INTRODUCTION: Peter Addyman, "Eburacum, Jorvik, York," *Scientific American*, March 1980; Arthur Cottrell, editor, *The Encyclopedia of Ancient Civilizations*; Roman Ghirshman, *The Arts of Ancient Iran*; Kathleen Kenyon, *Digging Up Jericho*; Irving Stone, *The Greek Treasure*; Sir Mortimer Wheeler, *Archaeology From the Earth*. THE SUMERIANS OF MESOPOTAMIA: Brian Fagan, *Return To Babylon*; Samuel Noah Kramer, *History Begins at Sumer* and *The Sumerians*; Nicholas Postgate, *The First Empires*; Georges Roux, *Ancient Iraq*; Sir Leonard Woolley, *Excavations at Ur*; Gavin Young and Nik Wheeler, *Return to the Marshes*. THE ROYAL CITIES OF SOLOMON: Michael Avi-Yonah, *Encyclopedia of Archaeological Excavations in the Holy Land*; Kathleen Kenyon, *Digging Up Jerusalem* and *Royal Cities of the Old Testament*; Magnus Magnusson, *Archaeology of the Bible*; James B. Pritchard, editor, *Solomon and Sheba*; Yigael Yadin, *Hazor*. POMPEII:

CITY SEALED IN TIME: Wilhelmina F. Jashemski, *The Gardens of Pompeii, Herculaneum, and the Villas Destroyed by Vesuvius*; Amedeo Maiuri, *Pompeii*; August Mau, *Pompeii: Its Life and Art*; THE MYSTERIOUS KINGDOM OF KUSH: William Y. Adams, *Nubia: Corridor to Africa*; *Africa in Antiquity: The Arts of Ancient Nubia and the Sudan*, published by the Brooklyn Museum; Peter L. Shinnie, *Meroe: A Civilization of the Sudan*. ANGKOR AND THE ANCIENT KHMER: John Audric, *Angkor and the Khmer Empire*; Madeleine Giteau, *The Civilization of Angkor*; Bernard P. Groslier and Jacques Arthaud, *Angkor: Art and Civilization*; Miroslav Krasa, *The Temples of Angkor*; Christopher Pym, editor, *Henri Mouhot's Diary*. THE HITTITES OF ASIA MINOR: Ekrem Akurgal, *The Art of the Hittites*; Kurt Bittel, *Hattusha* and *Les Hittites*; Oliver R. Gurney, *The Hittites*. LAND OF THE SINHALESE KINGS: Roloff Beny, *Island Ceylon*; E.F.C. Ludowyk, *The Footprint of Buddha* and *The Story of Ceylon*; Walpola Rahula, *History of Buddhism in Ceylon*; James Emerson Tennant, *Ceylon*.

Composition for *Splendors of the Past: Lost Cities of the Ancient World* by Composition Systems Inc., Arlington, Va., and National Geographic's Photographic Services (index pages). Printed by Federated Lithographers-Printers, Inc., Providence, R.I.; Holladay-Tyler Printing Corp., Rockville, Md.; and R. R. Donnelley & Sons Co., Crawfordsville, Ind. Bound by R. R. Donnelley & Sons Co. Color separations by The Lanman Companies, Washington, D. C.; Lincoln Graphics, Inc., Cherry Hill, N.J.; and Nashville Electrographics Corp., Nashville, Tenn.

Library of Congress CIP Data
Main entry under title:

Splendors of the past.

Bibliography: p.
Includes index.
1. Cities and towns, Ruined, extinct, etc.
2. Civilization, Ancient.   I. National Geographic Society (U. S.). Special Publications Division.
CB311.S735   930   80-7827
ISBN 0-87044-358-5   AACR2